THE EDEXCEL ANTHOLOGY FOR GCSE ENGLISH

ENGLISH 1203/1204 ENGLISH LITERATURE 1213

Hodder & Stoughton

A MEMBER OF THE HODDER HEADLINE GROUP

Acknowledgements

The publishers would like to thank the following for their kind permission to reproduce copyright material:

Copyright Photographs:

p1 two boys playing hide and seek © Nicola Sutton/Life File; p2 U.A. Fanthorpe, reproduced by permission of Penguin Books; p3 photograph of Jackie Kay © Jerry Bauer/Bloodaxe Books; p10 Oxford Street, bus queue, London, UK © Jeremy Hoare/Life File; p12 Prepared for War © Hulton Getty; p13 A French soldier's grave, marked by his rifle and helmet, on the battlefield of Verdun, circa 1916 © Hulton Getty; p18 photograph of Seamus Heaney, January 1997 © Stefan Rousseau/PA Photos; p21 man digging peat, Southern Ireland © Corbis; p26 *St George and the Dragon* by Uccello, reproduced by permission of the National Gallery, London; p30 a horse grazing © Emma Lee/Life File; p35 photograph of Ted Hughes © PA Photos; p38 Galapagos Land Iguana on South Plaza Island © Nigel Sitwell/Life File; p46 © Imperial War Museum; p47 child in Mongolian costume © Corbis; p53 Yorkshire moors © Corbis; p68 sunset © Corel; p81 cadillac © Corbis.

Copyright Text:

Isabel Allende: pp75–78 *The Schoolteacher's Guest* © Isabel Allende.
Moniza Alvi: p23 *An Unknown Girl* by Moniza Alvi from *Changing my Wife*, Bloodaxe Books, 2000.
Maya Angelou: p27 *Still I Rise* © Maya Angelou, 1969, taken from Virago Press Edition published by arrangement with The Random House Group.
W.H. Auden: p15 *Refugee Blues* from *Collected Poems*, reproduced by kind permission of Faber and Faber Ltd.
Alan Bennett: pp55–57 an extract from *Writing Home* © Alan Bennett, reproduced by permission of Faber and Faber Ltd.
John Betjeman: p8 *Death in Leamington* © John Betjeman, reproduced by permission of John Murray on behalf of the author.
Wendy Berliner: pp62–63 'Mind games' by Wendy Berliner, *The Guardian*, Tuesday August 14 2001 © Wendy Berliner.
Julian Borger: p61 'School sports culture leads to violence' by Julian Borger, Washington DC dispatch, *The Guardian*, Tuesday March 27 2001 © *The Guardian*.
Madeleine Bunting: p65 'Use persuasion not coercion' by Madeleine Bunting, *The Guardian*, Friday September 7 2001 © *The Guardian*.
Gillian Clarke: p17 *Miracle on St David's Day* © Gillian Clarke from *Collected Poems*, reproduced by permission of Carcanet Press.
Merle Collins: p10 *Where the Scattering Began* © Merle Collins, reproduced by permission of Virago Press.
Marcia Douglas: p9 *Electricity Comes to Cocoa Bottom* © Marcia Douglas 1999, reproduced by permission of the author and Peepal Tree Press.
U.A. Fanthorpe: p2 *Half-past Two* from *Neck Verse*, 1992 © U.A. Fanthorpe, reproduced by permission of the publishers, Peterloo Poets; p7 *You Will Be Hearing From Us Shortly* from *Standing To*, 1982 © U.A. Fanthorpe, reproduced by permission of the publishers, Peterloo Poets; pp25-26 *Not My Best Side* from *Side Effects*, 1978 © U.A. Fanthorpe, reproduced by permission of the publishers, Peterloo Poets; p32 *Old Man, Old Man* from *A Watching Brief*, 1987 © U.A. Fanthorpe, reproduced by permission of the publishers, Peterloo Poets.
Alexandra Frean: p64 'Liberal generation discovers discipline' by Alexandra Frean, *The Times*, Saturday April 3 1999.
Robert Frost: p28 *The Road Not Taken* from *The Poetry of Robert Frost*, edited by Edward Connery Latham, the Estate of Robert Frost and Jonathon Cape as publisher. Used by permission of The Random House Group Limited.
Nadine Gordimer: pp67–71 *Country Lovers* by Nadine Gordimer, by kind permission of A.P. Watt on behalf of the author.
Thomas Hardy: p16 *The Darkling Thrush;* p44 *The Five Students*.
John Harris: p60 'Save our children from the horrors of school sport' by John Harris, *The Independent*, Wednesday March 1 2000.
Seamus Heaney: p18 *Death of a Naturalist* from *Opened Ground*, 1998 © Seamus Heaney, reproduced by permission of Faber and Faber Ltd; p19 *The Barn* from *Opened Ground*, 1998 © Seamus Heaney, reproduced by permission of Faber and Faber Ltd; p20 *Follower* from *Opened Ground*, 1998 © Seamus Heaney, reproduced by permission of Faber and Faber Ltd; p21 *Digging* from *Opened Ground*, 1998 © Seamus Heaney, reproduced by permission of Faber and Faber Ltd; p22 *Mid-Term Break* from *Opened Ground*, 1998 © Seamus Heaney, reproduced by permission of Faber and Faber Ltd; p45 *Trout* from *Death of a Naturalist* © Seamus Heaney, reproduced by permission of Faber and Faber Ltd.

British Library Cataloguing in Publication Data
A catalogue record for this title is available from The British Library

ISBN 0 340 85726 9

First published 2002
Impression number 10 9 8 7 6 5 4 3 2 1
Year 2008 2007 2006 2005 2004 2003 2002

Edexcel Foundation, Stewart House, 32 Russell Square, London WC1B 5DN

Cover illustration by Stewart Larking.
Typeset by Fakenham Photosetting Limited, Fakenham, Norfolk.
Printed in Great Britain for Hodder & Stoughton Educational, a division of Hodder Headline Plc, 338 Euston Road, London NW1 3BH by Scotprint.

Contents

1 **Modern Poetry** for English Paper 2F or 4H, and English Literature Paper 2F or 3H

Collection A: **In Such a Time as This**

This collection includes poems which have a distinctive sense of time and place. The poems show people at different moments in their lives, responding to ordinary or extraordinary events.

Collection B: **Identity**

This collection focuses on the growth of an individual and how people develop and change throughout their lives. It explores how we relate to others and how others see us.

Collection C: **Nature**

This collection concerns responses to the natural world and how writers use nature as a source of emotions and ideas.

2 **Non-fiction prose** pieces for GCSE English A (1203), Paper 2F or 4H

3 **Different Cultures and Traditions** for GCSE English B (1204) Paper 2F or 4H

Short stories

1 Modern Poetry

Collection A: **In Such a Time as This**

Hide and Seek

Call out. Call loud: 'I'm ready! Come and find me!'
The sacks in the toolshed smell like the seaside.
They'll never find you in this salty dark,
But be careful that your feet aren't sticking out.
Wiser not to risk another shout.
The floor is cold. They'll probably be searching
The bushes near the swing. Whatever happens
You mustn't sneeze when they come prowling in.
And here they are, whispering at the door;
You've never heard them sound so hushed before.
Don't breathe. Don't move. Stay dumb. Hide in your blindness.
They're moving closer, someone stumbles, mutters;
Their words and laughter scuffle, and they're gone.
But don't come out just yet; they'll try the lane
And then the greenhouse and back here again.
They must be thinking that you're very clever,
Getting more puzzled as they search all over.
It seems a long time since they went away.
Your legs are stiff, the cold bites through your coat;
The dark damp smell of sand moves in your throat.
It's time to let them know that you're the winner.
Push off the sacks. Uncurl and stretch. That's better!
Out of the shed and call to them: 'I've won!
Here I am! Come and own up I've caught you!'
The darkening garden watches. Nothing stirs.
The bushes hold their breath; the sun is gone.
Yes, here you are. But where are they who sought you?

Vernon Scannell

Half-past Two

Once upon a schooltime
He did Something Very Wrong
(I forget what it was).

And She said he'd done
Something Very Wrong, and must
Stay in the school-room till half-past two.

(Being cross, she'd forgotten
She hadn't taught him Time.
He was too scared of being wicked to remind her.)

He knew a lot of time: he knew
Gettinguptime, timeyouwereofftime,
Timetogohomenowtime, TVtime,

Timeformykisstime (that was Grantime).
All the important times he knew,
But not half-past two.

He knew the clockface, the little eyes
And two long legs for walking,
But he couldn't click its language,

So he waited, beyond onceupona,
Out of reach of all the timefors,
And knew he'd escaped for ever

Into the smell of old chrysanthemums on Her desk,
Into the silent noise his hangnail made,
Into the air outside the window, into ever.

And then, *My goodness*, she said,
Scuttling in, *I forgot all about you.*
Run along or you'll be late.

So she slotted him back into schooltime,
And he got home in time for teatime,
Nexttime, notimeforthatnowtime,

But he never forgot how once by not knowing time,
He escaped into the clockless land of ever,
Where time hides tick-less waiting to be born.

U.A. Fanthorpe

Yellow

The hedge has its hair cut and stands between us
and the neighbours. The crocuses' yellow tongues
try to talk. The yellow bird in the birdcage is let out –
sometimes it flies alarmingly into my nest of hair.
I dream of budgies born in my curls. My mother
takes the yellow-and-white checked tea towel
from the kitchen and weeps into it before
drying the dishes; but she never cries into
the tea towel that is the map of New Zealand,
the south island, the north island, Christchurch, Wellington.
Never weeps into that one. My father, on the phone,
barks at cowardly comrades, *Now look here Comrade!* My brother
plays his flute in between chirping *Not listening Not listening.*

When my aunt Peggy comes from Edinburgh, she shoves my head
into a runny yellow yolk and says, *Don't be fussy! Get that down you!*
When my grandmother comes, my mother rushes up the stairs
and throws up in the bathroom. When my grandmother leaves,
my mother says, 'She always has that effect on me.'
Then we eat, my mother and I, her on her empty stomach,
eat what she calls a *plate*, 'Shall we make a plate?
Cheer ourselves up?' The plate has passionate beetroot balls
rolling across it, a piece of Edam because it's slimming,
a slice of ham, a happy yellow pineapple ring.
Two white sweet pickled onions stare like blind eyes.

Jackie Kay

Brendon Gallacher

He was seven and I was six, my Brendon Gallacher.
He was Irish and I was Scottish, my Brendon Gallacher.
His father was in prison; he was a cat burglar.
My father was communist party full-time worker.
He had six brothers and I had one, my Brendon Gallacher.

He would hold my hand and take me by the river
where we'd talk all about his family being poor.
He'd get his mum out of Glasgow when he got older.
A wee holiday some place nice. Some place far.
I'd tell my mum about my Brendon Gallacher.

How his mum drank and his daddy was a cat burglar.
And she'd say, 'why not have him round to dinner?'
No, no, I'd say he's got big holes in his trousers.
I like meeting him by the burn in the open air.
Then one day after we'd been friends for two years,

One day when it was pouring and I was indoors,
my mum says to me, 'I was talking to Mrs Moir
who lives next door to your Brendon Gallacher
Didn't you say his address was 24 Novar?
She says there are no Gallachers at 24 Novar

There never have been any Gallachers next door.'
And he died then, my Brendon Gallacher,
flat out on my bedroom floor, his spiky hair,
his impish grin, his funning flapping ear.
O Brendon. Oh my Brendon Gallacher.

Jackie Kay

Lucozade

My mum is on a high bed next to the sad chrysanthemums.
'Don't bring flowers, they only wilt and die.'
I am scared my mum is going to die
on the bed next to the sad chrysanthemums.

She nods off and her eyes go back in her head.
Next to her bed is a bottle of Lucozade.
'Orange nostalgia, that's what that is,' she says.
'Don't bring Lucozade either,' then fades.

'The whole day was a blur, a swarm of eyes.
Those doctors with their white lies.
Did you think you could cheer me up with a *Woman's Own*?
Don't bring magazines, too much about size.'

My mum wakes up, groggy and low.
'What I want to know,' she says, 'is this:
where's the big brandy, the generous gin, the Bloody Mary,
the biscuit tin, the chocolate gingers, the dirty big meringue?'

I am sixteen; I've never tasted a Bloody Mary.
'Tell your father to bring a luxury,' says she.
'Grapes have no imagination, they're just green.
Tell him: stop the neighbours coming.'

I clear her cupboard in ward 10B, Stobhill Hospital.
I leave, bags full, Lucozade, grapes, oranges,
sad chrysanthemums under my arms,
weighted down. I turn round, wave with her flowers.

My mother, on her high hospital bed, waves back.
Her face is light and radiant, dandelion hours.
Her sheets billow and whirl. She is beautiful.
Next to her the empty table is divine.

I carry the orange nostalgia home singing an old song.

Jackie Kay

The House

The house had a dozen bedrooms,
each of them cold, and the wind
battered the windows and blew down
power-lines to leave the house dark.
Rats lived in the foundations,
sending scouts under the stairs
for a year or two, and once
a friendly ghost was glimpsed
at the foot of a bed. Downhill
half a mile was the Atlantic,
with its ration of the drowned –
one of whom visited the house,
carried there on a door.
It hosted dry corpses, too,
with nostrils huge to a child,
but never a murder –
except the lambs bled dry
in the yard outside. Sunlight
never took over the interior,
and after dark the cockroaches
came from under a cupboard
to be eaten by the dog.
Crows were always sitting
on the wires, planning nests
in the chimneys, and a shotgun
sometimes blew a few away.
Neighbours never entered
as often as in other houses,
but it did have a piano upstairs.
And I did grow up there.

Matthew Sweeney

You Will Be Hearing From Us Shortly

You feel adequate to the demands of this position?
What qualities do you feel you
Personally have to offer?

Ah

Let us consider your application form.
Your qualifications, though impressive are
Not, we must admit, precisely what
We had in mind. Would you care
To defend their relevance?

Indeed

Now your age. Perhaps you feel able
To make your own comment about that,
Too? We are conscious ourselves
Of the need for a candidate with precisely
The right degree of immaturity.

So glad we agree

And now a delicate matter: your looks.
You do appreciate this work involves
Contact with the actual public? Might they,
Perhaps, find your appearance
Disturbing?

Quite so

And your accent. That is the way
You have always spoken, is it? What
Of your education? Were
You educated? We mean, of course,
Where were you educated?
And how
Much of a handicap is that to you,
Would you say?

Married, children,
We see. The usual dubious
Desire to perpetuate what had better
Not have happened at all. We do not
Ask what domestic disasters shimmer
Behind that vaguely unsuitable address.

And you were born – ?

Yes. Pity.

So glad we agree.

U.A. Fanthorpe

Death in Leamington

She died in the upstairs bedroom
   By the light of the ev'ning star
That shone through the plate glass window
   From over Leamington Spa.

Beside her the lonely crochet
   Lay patiently and unstirred,
But the fingers that would have work'd it
   Were dead as the spoken word.

And Nurse came in with the tea-things
   Breast high 'mid the stands and chairs –
But Nurse was alone with her own little soul,
   And the things were alone with theirs.

She bolted the big round window,
   She let the blinds unroll,
She set a match to the mantle,
   She covered the fire with coal.

And 'Tea!' she said in a tiny voice
   'Wake up! It's nearly *five*.'
Oh! Chintzy, chintzy cheeriness,
   Half dead and half alive!

Do you know that the stucco is peeling?
   Do you know that the heart will stop?
From those yellow Italianate arches
   Do you hear the plaster drop?

Nurse looked at the silent bedstead,
   At the gray, decaying face,
As the calm of a Leamington ev'ning
   Drifted into the place.

She moved the table of bottles
   Away from the bed to the wall,
And tiptoeing gently over the stairs
   Turned down the gas in the hall.

John Betjeman

Electricity Comes to Cocoa Bottom

Then all the children of Cocoa Bottom
went to see Mr. Samuel's electric lights.
They camped on the grass bank outside his house,
their lamps filled with oil,
waiting for sunset,
watching the sky turn yellow, orange.
Grannie Patterson across the road
peeped through the crack in her porch door.
The cable was drawn like a pencil line across the sun.
The fireflies waited in the shadows,
their lanterns off.
The kling-klings swooped in from the hills,
congregating in the orange trees.
A breeze coming home from sea held its breath;
bamboo lining the dirt road stopped its swaying,
and evening came as soft as chiffon curtains:
Closing. Closing.

Light!
Mr. Samuel smiling on the verandah –
a silhouette against the yellow shimmer behind him –
and there arising such a gasp,
such a fluttering of wings,
tweet-a-whit,
such a swaying, swaying.
Light! Marvellous light!
And then the breeze rose up from above the trees,
swelling and swelling into a wind
such that the long grass bent forward
stretching across the bank like so many bowed heads.
And a voice in the wind whispered:
Is there one among us to record this moment?
But there was none –

no one (except for a few warm rocks
hidden among mongoose ferns) even heard a sound.
Already the children of Cocoa Bottom
had lit their lamps for the dark journey home,
and it was too late –
the moment had passed.

Marcia Douglas

Glossary: *Kling-klings* – birds

Where the Scattering Began

Here, on the streets of London
where, some say, the scattering began
we come to find our faces again
We come to measure the rhythm of our paces
against the call of the Ghanaian drum that talks
against the wail of the mbira from Zimbabwe
that yields music to the thumbs
We come with faces denying names
gone English, Irish, Scottish
We come with hands that speak
in ways the tongue has forgotten
We come with intonations
that reshape languages we have been given
We come with eyes that tell a story
the brain cannot recall
We come with the blue of the sea so close
that we lift our eyes with yearning
to the emptiness of the skies
Some of us come with the memory of
forest sounds that we have never known
We all come speaking so simply
of complicated things. Here
when we recognize each other
on the streets of London
hands and eyes and ears
begin to shape answers
to questions tongue can find
no words for asking.

Merle Collins

Glossary: *mbira* – musical instrument

Wherever I Hang

I leave me people, me land, me home
For reasons, I not too sure
I forsake de sun
And de humming-bird splendour
Had big rats in de floorboard
So I pick up me new-world-self
And come, to this place call England
At first I feeling like I in dream –
De misty greyness
I touching de walls to see if they real
They solid to de seam
And de people pouring from de underground system
Like beans
And when I look up to de sky
I see Lord Nelson high – too high to lie

And is so I sending home photos of myself
Among de pigeons and de snow
And is so I warding off de cold
And is so, little by little
I begin to change my calypso ways
Never visiting nobody
Before giving them clear warning
And waiting me turn in queue
Now, after all this time
I get accustom to de English life
But I still miss back-home side
To tell you de truth
I don't know really where I belaang

Yes, divided to de ocean
Divided to de bone

Wherever I hang me knickers – that's my home.

Grace Nichols

The Send-off

Down the close, darkening lanes they sang their way
To the siding-shed,
And lined the train with faces grimly gay.

Their breasts were stuck all white with wreath and spray
As men's are, dead.

Dull porters watched them, and a casual tramp
Stood staring hard,
Sorry to miss them from the upland camp.
Then, unmoved, signals nodded, and a lamp
Winked to the guard.

So secretly, like wrongs hushed-up, they went.
They were not ours:
We never heard to which front these were sent.

Nor there if they yet mock what women meant
Who gave them flowers.

Shall they return to beatings of great bells
In wild train-loads?
A few, a few, too few for drums and yells,
May creep back, silent, to village wells
Up half-known roads.

Wilfred Owen

Dulce et Decorum Est

Bent double, like old beggars under sacks,
Knock-kneed, coughing like hags, we cursed through sludge,
Till on the haunting flares we turned our backs,
And towards our distant rest began to trudge.
Men marched asleep. Many had lost their boots,
But limped on, blood-shod. All went lame, all blind;
Drunk with fatigue; deaf even to the hoots
Of gas-shells dropping softly behind.

Gas! Gas! Quick, boys! — An ecstasy of fumbling,
Fitting the clumsy helmets just in time,
But someone still was yelling out and stumbling
And floundering like a man in fire or lime.—
Dim through the misty panes and thick green light,
As under a green sea, I saw him drowning.

In all my dreams before my helpless sight
He plunges at me, guttering, choking, drowning.

If in some smothering dreams, you too could pace
Behind the wagon that we flung him in,
And watch the white eyes writhing in his face,
His hanging face, like a devil's sick of sin;
If you could hear, at every jolt, the blood
Come gargling from the froth-corrupted lungs,
Bitter as the cud
Of vile, incurable sores on innocent tongues,—
My friend, you would not tell with such high zest
To children ardent for some desperate glory,
The old Lie: Dulce et decorum est
Pro patria mori.

Wilfred Owen

From War Music

This extract describes an incident from the siege of Troy, adapted in modern English from Homer's epic poem *The Iliad*.

At this moment the Trojans have the upper hand. They have driven the Greeks back to the beach, and threaten to burn their ships.

The Greek warrior Ajax, physically massive but slow at thought, is taunted here by Prince Hector of Troy.

Cut to the Fleet.

The air near Ajax was so thick with arrows, that,
As they came, their shanks tickered against each other;
And under them the Trojans swarmed so thick
Ajax outspread his arms, turned his spear flat,
And simply *pushed*. Yet they came clamouring back until
So many Trojans had a go at him
The iron chaps of Ajax' helmet slapped his cheeks
To soft red pulp, and his head reached back and forth
Like a clapper inside a bell made out of sword blades.
Maybe, even with no breath left,
Big Ajax might have stood it yet; yet
Big and all as he was, Prince Hector meant to burn that ship:
And God was pleased to let him.

Pulling the Trojans out a yard or two,
He baited Ajax with his throat; and Ajax took.
As the spear lifted, Hector skipped in range;
As Ajax readied, Hector bared his throat again;
And, as Ajax lunged, Prince Hector jived on his right heel
And snicked the haft clean through its neck,
Pruning the bronze nose off — Aie! — it was good to watch
Big Ajax and his spear, both empty topped,
Blundering about for — Oh, a minute went
Before he noticed it had gone.
But when he noticed it he knew
God stood by Hector's elbow, not by his;
That God was pleased with Hector, not with Ajax;
And, sensibly enough, he fled.

The ship was burned.

Christopher Logue

Refugee Blues

Say this city has ten million souls,
Some are living in mansions, some are living in holes:
Yet there's no place for us, my dear, yet there's no place for us.

Once we had a country and we thought it fair,
Look in the atlas and you'll find it there:
We cannot go there now, my dear, we cannot go there now.

In the village churchyard there grows an old yew,
Every spring it blossoms anew:
Old passports can't do that, my dear, old passports can't do that.

The consul banged the table and said,
"If you've got no passport you're officially dead":
But we are still alive, my dear, but we are still alive.

Went to a committee; they offered me a chair;
Asked me politely to return next year:
But where shall we go to-day, my dear, but where shall we go to-day?

Came to a public meeting; the speaker got up and said:
"If we let them in, they will steal our daily bread":
He was talking of you and me, my dear, he was talking of you and me.

Thought I heard the thunder rumbling in the sky;
It was Hitler over Europe, saying, "They must die":
O we were in his mind, my dear, O we were in his mind.

Saw a poodle in a jacket fastened with a pin,
Saw a door opened and a cat let in:
But they weren't German Jews, my dear, but they weren't German Jews.

Went down the harbour and stood upon the quay,
Saw the fish swimming as if they were free:
Only ten feet away, my dear, only ten feet away.

Walked through a wood, saw the birds in the trees;
They had no politicians and sang at their ease:
They weren't the human race, my dear, they weren't the human race.

Dreamed I saw a building with a thousand floors,
A thousand windows and a thousand doors:
Not one of them was ours, my dear, not one of them was ours.

Stood on a great plain in the falling snow;
Ten thousand soldiers marched to and fro:
Looking for you and me, my dear, looking for you and me.

W.H. Auden

The Darkling Thrush

I leant upon a coppice gate
   When Frost was spectre-gray,
And Winter's dregs made desolate
The weakening eye of day.
The tangled bine-stems scored the sky
   Like strings of broken lyres,
And all mankind that haunted nigh
   Had sought their household fires.

The land's sharp features seemed to be
   The Century's corpse outleant,
His crypt the cloudy canopy,
   The wind his death-lament.
The ancient pulse of germ and birth
   Was shrunken hard and dry,
And every spirit upon earth
   Seemed fervourless as I.

At once a voice arose among
   The bleak twigs overhead
In a full-hearted evensong
   Of joy illimited;
An aged thrush, frail, gaunt, and small,
   In black-beruffled plume,
Had chosen thus to fling his soul
   Upon the growing gloom.

So little cause for carolings
   Of such ecstatic sound
Was written on terrestrial things
   Afar or nigh around,
That I could think there trembled through
   His happy good-night air
Some blessed Hope, whereof he knew
   And I was unaware.

31 December 1900

Thomas Hardy

Miracle on St David's Day

"They flash upon that inward eye
Which is the bliss of solitude"
The Daffodils by W. Wordsworth

An afternoon yellow and open-mouthed
with daffodils. The sun treads the path
among cedars and enormous oaks.
It might be a country house, guests strolling,
the rumps of gardeners between nursery shrubs.

I am reading poetry to the insane.
An old woman, interrupting, offers
as many buckets of coal as I need.
A beautiful chestnut-haired boy listens
entirely absorbed. A schizophrenic

on a good day, they tell me later.
In a cage of first March sun a woman
sits not listening, not seeing, not feeling.
In her neat clothes the woman is absent.
A big, mild man is tenderly led

to his chair. He has never spoken.
His labourer's hands on his knees, he rocks
gently to the rhythms of the poems.
I read to their presences, absences,
to the big, dumb labouring man as he rocks.

He is suddenly standing, silently,
huge and mild, but I feel afraid. Like slow
movement of spring water or the first bird
of the year in the breaking darkness,
the labourer's voice recites "The Daffodils".

The nurses are frozen, alert; the patients
seem to listen. He is hoarse but word-perfect.
Outside the daffodils are still as wax,
a thousand, ten thousand, their syllables
unspoken, their creams and yellows still.

Forty years ago, in a Valleys school,
the class recited poetry by rote.
Since the dumbness of misery fell
he has remembered there was a music
of speech and that once he had something to say.

When he's done, before the applause, we observe
the flowers' silence. A thrush sings
and the daffodils are flame.

Gillian Clarke

Death of a Naturalist

All year the flax-dam festered in the heart
Of the townland; green and heavy headed
Flax had rotted there, weighted down by huge sods.
Daily it sweltered in the punishing sun.
Bubbles gargled delicately, bluebottles
Wove a strong gauze of sound around the smell.
There were dragon-flies, spotted butterflies,
But best of all was the warm thick slobber
Of frogspawn that grew like clotted water
In the shade of the banks. Here, every spring
I would fill jampotfuls of the jellied
Specks to range on window-sills at home,
On shelves at school, and wait and watch until
The fattening dots burst into nimble
Swimming tadpoles. Miss Walls would tell us how
The daddy frog was called a bullfrog
And how he croaked and how the mammy frog
Laid hundreds of little eggs and this was
Frogspawn. You could tell the weather by frogs too
For they were yellow in the sun and brown
In rain.

Then one hot day when fields were rank
With cowdung in the grass the angry frogs
Invaded the flax-dam; I ducked through hedges
To a coarse croaking that I had not heard
Before. The air was thick with a bass chorus.
Right down the dam gross-bellied frogs were cocked
On sods; their loose necks pulsed like sails. Some hopped:
The slap and plop were obscene threats. Some sat
Poised like mud grenades, their blunt heads farting.
I sickened, turned, and ran. The great slime kings
Were gathered there for vengeance and I knew
That if I dipped my hand the spawn would clutch it.

Seamus Heaney

The Barn

Threshed corn lay piled like grit of ivory
Or solid as cement in two-lugged sacks.
The musty dark hoarded an armoury
Of farmyard implements, harness, plough-socks.

The floor was mouse-grey, smooth, chilly concrete.
There were no windows, just two narrow shafts
Of gilded motes, crossing, from air-holes slit
High in each gable. The one door meant no draughts

All summer when the zinc burned like an oven.
A scythe's edge, a clean spade, a pitch-fork's prongs:
Slowly bright objects formed when you went in.
Then you felt cobwebs clogging up your lungs

And scuttled fast into the sunlit yard.
And into nights when bats were on the wing
Over the rafters of sleep, where bright eyes stared
From piles of grain in corners, fierce, unblinking.

The dark gulfed like a roof-space. I was chaff
To be pecked up when birds shot through the air-slits.
I lay face-down to shun the fear above.
The two-lugged sacks moved in like great blind rats.

Seamus Heaney

Follower

My father worked with a horse-plough,
His shoulders globed like a full sail strung
Between the shafts and the furrow.
The horses strained at his clicking tongue.

An expert. He would set the wing
And fit the bright steel-pointed sock.
The sod rolled over without breaking.
At the headrig, with a single pluck

Of reins, the sweating team turned round
And back into the land. His eye
Narrowed and angled at the ground
Mapping the furrow exactly.

I stumbled in his hob-nailed wake,
Fell sometimes on the polished sod;
Sometimes he rode me on his back
Dipping and rising to his plod.

I wanted to grow up and plough,
To close one eye, stiffen my arm.
All I ever did was follow
In his broad shadow round the farm.

I was a nuisance, tripping, falling,
Yapping always. But today
It is my father who keeps stumbling
Behind me, and will not go away.

Seamus Heaney

Digging

Between my finger and my thumb
The squat pen rests; snug as a gun.

Under my window, a clean rasping sound
When the spade sinks into gravelly ground:
My father, digging. I look down

Till his straining rump among the flowerbeds
Bends low, comes up twenty years away
Stooping in rhythm through potato drills
Where he was digging.

The coarse boot nestled on the lug, the shaft
Against the inside knee was levered firmly.
He rooted out tall tops, buried the bright edge deep
To scatter new potatoes that we picked
Loving their cool hardness in our hands.

By God, the old man could handle a spade.
Just like his old man.

My grandfather cut more turf in a day
Than any other man on Toner's bog.
Once I carried him milk in a bottle
Corked sloppily with paper. He straightened up
To drink it, then fell to right away
Nicking and slicing neatly, heaving sods
Over his shoulder, going down and down
For the good turf. Digging.

The cold smell of potato mould, the squelch and slap
Of soggy peat, the curt cuts of an edge
Through living roots awaken in my head.
But I've no spade to follow men like them.

Between my finger and my thumb
The squat pen rests.
I'll dig with it.

Seamus Heaney

Mid-Term Break

I sat all morning in the college sick bay
Counting bells knelling classes to a close.
At two o'clock our neighbours drove me home.

In the porch I met my father crying –
He had always taken funerals in his stride –
And Big Jim Evans saying it was a hard blow.

The baby cooed and laughed and rocked the pram
When I came in, and I was embarrassed
By old men standing up to shake my hand

And tell me they were 'sorry for my trouble'.
Whispers informed strangers I was the eldest,
Away at school, as my mother held my hand

In hers and coughed out angry tearless sighs.
At ten o'clock the ambulance arrived
With the corpse, stanched and bandaged by the nurses.

Next morning I went up into the room. Snowdrops
And candles soothed the bedside. I saw him
For the first time in six weeks. Paler now,

Wearing a poppy bruise on his left temple,
He lay in the four foot box as in his cot.
No gaudy scars, the bumper knocked him clear.

A four foot box, a foot for every year.

Seamus Heaney

An Unknown Girl

In the evening bazaar
studded with neon
an unknown girl
is hennaing my hand.
She squeezes a wet brown line
from a nozzle.
She is icing my hand.
which she steadies with hers
on her satin-peach knee.
In the evening bazaar
for a few rupees
an unknown girl
is hennaing my hand.
As a little air catches
my shadow-stitched kameez
a peacock spreads its lines
across my palm.
Colours leave the street
float up in balloons.
Dummies in shop-fronts
tilt and stare
with their Western perms.
Banners for Miss India 1993.
for curtain cloth
and sofa cloth
canopy me.
I have new brown veins.
In the evening bazaar
very deftly
an unknown girl
is hennaing my hand.
I am clinging
to these firm peacock lines
like people who cling
to the sides of a train.
Now the furious streets
are hushed.
I'll scrape off
the dry brown lines
before I sleep.
reveal soft as a snail trail
the amber bird beneath.
It will fade in a week.
When India appears and reappears
I'll lean across a country
with my hands outstretched
longing for the unknown girl
in the neon bazaar.

Moniza Alvi

Glossary: *hennaing* – art of body decoration using a plant dye
kameez – loose fitting tunic

Once Upon a Time

Once upon a time, son,
they used to laugh with their hearts
and laugh with their eyes:
but now they only laugh with their teeth,
while their ice-block cold eyes
search behind my shadow.

There was a time indeed
they used to shake hands with their hearts:
but that's gone, son.
Now they shake hands without hearts
while their left hands search
my empty pockets.

'Feel at home'! 'Come again':
they say, and when I come
again and feel
at home, once, twice,
there will be no thrice –
for then I find doors shut on me.

So I have learned many things, son.
I have learned to wear many faces
like dresses – homeface,
officeface, streetface, hostface,
cocktailface, with all their conforming smiles
like a fixed portrait smile.

And I have learned too
to laugh with only my teeth
and shake hands without my heart.
I have also learned to say, 'Goodbye',
when I mean 'Good-riddance':
to say 'Glad to meet you',
without being glad; and to say 'It's been
nice talking to you', after being bored.

But believe me, son.
I want to be what I used to be
when I was like you. I want
to unlearn all these muting things.
Most of all, I want to relearn
how to laugh, for my laugh in the mirror
shows only my teeth like a snake's bare
fangs!

So show me, son,
how to laugh; show me how
I used to laugh and smile
once upon a time when I was like you.

Gabriel Okara

Not My Best Side

I

Not my best side, I'm afraid.
The artist didn't give me a chance to
Pose properly, and as you can see,
Poor chap, he had this obsession with
Triangles, so he left off two of my
Feet. I didn't comment at the time
(What, after all, are two feet
To a monster?) But afterwards
I was sorry for the bad publicity.
Why, I said to myself, should my conqueror
Be so ostentatiously beardless, and ride
A horse with a deformed neck and square hoofs?
Why should my victim be so
Unattractive as to be inedible,
And why should she have me literally
On a string? I don't mind dying
Ritually, since I always rise again,
But I should have liked a little more blood
To show they were taking me seriously.

II

It's hard for a girl to be sure if
She wants to be rescued. I mean, I quite
Took to the dragon. It's nice to be
Liked, if you know what I mean. He was
So nicely physical, with his claws
And lovely green skin, and that sexy tail,
And the way he looked at me,
He made me feel he was all ready to
Eat me. And any girl enjoys that.
So when this boy turned up, wearing machinery,
On a really dangerous horse, to be honest,
I didn't much fancy him. I mean,
What was he like underneath the hardware?
He might have acne, blackheads or even
Bad breath for all I could tell, but the dragon –
Well, you could see all his equipment
At a glance. Still, what could I do?
The dragon got himself beaten by the boy,
And a girl's got to think of her future.

III

I have diplomas in Dragon
Management and Virgin Reclamation.
My horse is the latest model with
Automatic transmission and built-in
Obsolescence. My spear is custom-built,
And my prototype armour
Still on the secret list. You can't

'This is based on Uccello's painting of St George and the Dragon [above], which you can see in the National Gallery in London. I thought it might be interesting to find voices for characters who are usually seen as conventionally good, bad, or helpless.'

Do better than me at the moment.
I'm qualified and equipped to the
Eyebrow. So why be difficult?
Don't you want to be killed and/or rescued
In the most contemporary way? Don't
You want to carry out the roles
That sociology and myth have designed for you?
Don't you realise that, by being choosy,
You are endangering job-prospects
In the spear- and horse-building industries?
What, in any case, does it matter what
You want? You're in my way.

U.A. Fanthorpe

Still I Rise

You may write me down in history
With your bitter, twisted lies.
You may trod me in the very dirt
But still, like dust, I'll rise.

Does my sassiness upset you?
Why are you beset with gloom?
'Cause I walk like I've got oil wells
Pumping in my living room.

Just like moons and like suns,
With the certainty of tides,
Just like hopes springing high,
Still I'll rise.

Did you want to see me broken?
Bowed head and lowered eyes?
Shoulders falling down like teardrops,
Weakened by my soulful cries.

Does my haughtiness offend you?
Don't you take it awful hard
'Cause I laugh like I've got gold mines
Diggin' in my own back yard.

You may shoot me with your words,
You may cut me with your eyes,
You may kill me with your hatefulness,
But still, like air, I'll rise.

Does my sexiness upset you?
Does it come as a surprise
That I dance like I've got diamonds
At the meeting of my thighs?

Out of the huts of history's shame
I rise
Up from a past that's rooted in pain
I rise
I'm a black ocean, leaping and wide,
Welling and swelling I bear in the tide.

Leaving behind nights of terror and fear
I rise
Into a daybreak that's wondrously clear
I rise
Being the gifts that my ancestors gave,
I am the dream and the hope of the slave.
I rise
I rise
I rise

Maya Angelou

The Road Not Taken

Two roads diverged in a yellow wood,
And sorry I could not travel both
And be one traveller, long I stood
And looked down one as far as I could
To where it bent in the undergrowth;

Then took the other, as just as fair,
And having perhaps the better claim,
Because it was grassy and wanted wear;
Though as for that the passing there
Had worn them really about the same.

And both that morning equally lay
In leaves no step had trodden black.
Oh, I kept the first for another day!
Yet knowing how way leads on to way,
I doubted if I should ever come back.

I shall be telling this with a sigh
Somewhere ages and ages hence;
Two roads diverged in a wood, and I –
I took the one less travelled by,
And that has made all the difference.

Robert Frost

Warning

When I am an old woman I shall wear purple
With a red hat which doesn't go, and doesn't suit me.
And I shall spend my pension on brandy and summer gloves
And satin sandals, and say we've no money for butter.
I shall sit down on the pavement when I'm tired
And gobble up samples in shops and press alarm bells
And run my stick along the public railings
And make up for the sobriety of my youth.
I shall go out in my slippers in the rain
And pick the flowers in other people's gardens
And learn to spit.

You can wear terrible shirts and grow more fat
And eat three pounds of sausages at a go
Or only bread and pickle for a week
And hoard pens and pencils and beermats and things in boxes.

But now we must have clothes that keep us dry
And pay our rent and not swear in the street
And set a good example for the children.
We must have friends to dinner and read the papers.

But maybe I ought to practise a little now?
So people who know me are not too shocked and surprised
When suddenly I am old, and start to wear purple.

Jenny Joseph

I Shall Paint my Nails Red

Because a bit of colour is a public service.
Because I am proud of my hands.
Because it will remind me I'm a woman.
Because I will look like a survivor.
Because I can admire them in traffic jams.
Because my daughter will say ugh.
Because my lover will be surprised.
Because it is quicker than dyeing my hair.
Because it is a ten-minute moratorium.
Because it is reversible.

Carole Satyamurti

At Grass

The eye can hardly pick them out
From the cold shade they shelter in,
Till wind distresses tail and mane;
Then one crops grass, and moves about
—The other seeming to look on—
And stands anonymous again.

Yet fifteen years ago, perhaps
Two dozen distances sufficed
To fable them: faint afternoons
Of Cups and Stakes and Handicaps,
Whereby their names were artificed
To inlay faded, classic Junes—

Silks at the start: against the sky
Numbers and parasols: outside,
Squadrons of empty cars, and heat,
And littered grass: then the long cry
Hanging unhushed till it subside
To stop-press columns on the street.

Do memories plague their ears like flies?
They shake their heads. Dusk brims the shadows.
Summer by summer all stole away,
The starting-gates, the crowds and cries—
All but the unmolesting meadows.
Almanacked, their names live; they

Have slipped their names, and stand at ease,
Or gallop for what must be joy,
And not a fieldglass sees them home,
Or curious stop-watch prophesies:
Only the groom, and the groom's boy,
With bridles in the evening come.

Philip Larkin

Mirror

I am silver and exact. I have no preconceptions.
Whatever I see I swallow immediately
Just as it is, unmisted by love or dislike.
I am not cruel, only truthful –
The eye of a little god, four-cornered.
Most of the time I meditate on the opposite wall.
It is pink, with speckles. I have looked at it so long
I think it is part of my heart. But it flickers.
Faces and darkness separate us over and over.

Now I am a lake. A woman bends over me,
Searching my reaches for what she really is.
Then she turns to those liars, the candles or the moon.
I see her back, and reflect it faithfully.
She rewards me with tears and an agitation of hands.
I am important to her. She comes and goes.
Each morning it is her face that replaces the darkness.
In me she has drowned a young girl, and in me an old woman
Rises towards her day after day, like a terrible fish.

Sylvia Plath

Old Man, Old Man

He lives in a world of small recalcitrant
Things in bottles, with tacky labels. He was always
A man who did-it-himself.

Now his hands shamble among clues
He left for himself when he saw better,
And small things distress: *I've lost the hammer.*

Lifelong adjuster of environments,
Lord once of shed, garage and garden,
Each with its proper complement of tackle,

World authority on twelve different
Sorts of glue, connoisseur of nuts
And bolts, not good with daughters

But a dab hand with the Black and Decker,
Self-demoted in your nineties to washing-up
After supper, and missing crusted streaks

Of food on plates; have you forgotten
The jokes you no longer tell, as you forget
If you've smoked your timetabled cigarette?

Now television has no power to arouse
Your surliness; your wife could replace on the walls
Those pictures of disinherited children,

And you wouldn't know. Now you ramble
In your talk around London districts, fretting
At how to find your way from Holborn to Soho,

And where is Drury Lane? Old man, old man,
So obdurate in your contracted world,
Living in almost-dark, *I can see you,*

You said to me, *but only as a cloud.*
When I left, you tried not to cry. I love
Your helplessness, you who hate being helpless.

Let me find your hammer. Let me
Walk with you to Drury Lane. I am only a cloud.

U.A. Fanthorpe

The Horses

Barely a twelvemonth after
The seven days war that put the world to sleep,
Late in the evening the strange horses came.
By then we had made our covenant with silence
But in the first few days it was so still
We listened to our breathing and were afraid.
On the second day
The radios failed; we turned the knobs; no answer.
On the third day a warship passed us, heading north,
Dead bodies piled on the deck. On the sixth day
A plane plunged over us into the sea. Thereafter
Nothing. The radios dumb:
And still they stand in corners of our kitchens,
And stand, perhaps, turned on, in a million rooms
All over the world. But now if they should speak,
If on a sudden they should speak again,
If on the stroke of noon a voice should speak,
We would not listen, we would not let it bring
That bad old world that swallowed its children quick
At one great gulp. We would not have it again.
Sometimes we think of the nations lying asleep,
Curled blindly in impenetrable sorrow,
And then the thought confounds us with its
strangeness.

The tractors lie about our fields; at evening
They look like dank sea-monsters crouched and
waiting.
We leave them where they are and let them rust:
'They'll moulder away and be like other loam.'
We make our oxen drag our rusty ploughs,
Long laid aside. We have gone back
Far past our fathers' land.
And then, that evening
Late in the summer the strange horses came.
We heard a distant tapping on the road,
A deepening drumming; it stopped, went on again,
And at the corner changed to hollow thunder.
We saw the heads
Like a wild wave charging and were afraid.
We had sold our horses in our fathers' time
To buy new tractors. Now they were strange to us
As fabulous steeds set on an ancient shield
Or illustrations in a book of knights.

continued

We did not dare go near them. Yet they waited,
Stubborn and shy, as if they had been sent
By an old command to find our whereabouts
And that long-lost archaic companionship.
In the first moment we had never a thought
That they were creatures to be owned and used.
Among them were some half-a-dozen colts
Dropped in some wilderness of the broken world,
Yet new as if they had come from their own Eden.
Since then they have pulled our ploughs and borne our loads,
But that free servitude still can pierce our hearts.
Our life is changed; their coming our beginning.

Edwin Muir

Wind

This house has been far out at sea all night,
The woods crashing through darkness, the booming hills
Winds stampeding the fields under the window
Floundering black astride and blinding wet

Till day rose; then under an orange sky
The hills had new places, and wind wielded
Blade-light, luminous black and emerald,
Flexing like the lens of a mad eye.

At noon I scaled along the house-side as far as
The coal-house door. I dared once to look up-
Through the brunt wind that dented the balls of my eyes
The tent of the hills drummed and strained its guyrope,

The fields quivering, the skyline a grimace,
At any second to bang and vanish with a flap:
The wind flung a magpie away and a black-
Back gull bent like an iron bar slowly. The house

Rang like some fine green goblet in the note
That any second would shatter it. Now deep
in chairs, in front of the great fire, we grip
Our hearts and cannot entertain book, thought

Or each other. We watch the fire blazing,
And feel the roots of the house move, but sit on
Seeing the window tremble to come in,
Hearing the stones cry out under the horizons.

Ted Hughes

The Thought-Fox

I imagine this midnight moment's forest:
Something else is alive
Beside the clock's loneliness
And this blank page where my fingers move.

Through the window I see no star:
Something more near
Though deeper within darkness
Is entering the loneliness:

Cold, delicately as the dark snow
A fox's nose touches twig, leaf;
Two eyes serve a movement, that now
And again now, and now, and now

Sets neat prints into the snow
Between trees, and warily a lame
Shadow lags by stump and in hollow
Of a body that is bold to come

Across clearings, an eye,
A widening deepening greenness,
Brilliantly, concentratedly,
Coming about its own business

Till, with a sudden sharp hot stink of fox
It enters the dark hole of the head.
The window is starless still; the clock ticks,
The page is printed.

Ted Hughes

The Stag

While the rain fell on the November woodland shoulder of Exmoor
While the traffic jam along the road honked and shouted
Because the farmers were parking wherever they could
And scrambling to the bank-top to stare through the tree-fringe
Which was leafless,
The stag ran through his private forest.

While the rain drummed on the roofs of the parked cars
And the kids inside cried and daubed their chocolate and fought
And mothers and aunts and grandmothers
Were a tangle of undoing sandwiches and screwed-round gossiping heads
Steaming up the windows,
The stag loped through his favourite valley.

While the blue horseman down in the boggy meadow
Sodden nearly black, on sodden horses,
Spaced as at a military parade,
Moved a few paces to the right and a few to the left and felt rather foolish
Looking at the brown impassable river,
The stag came over the last hill of Exmoor.

While everybody high-kneed it to the bank-top all along the road
Where steady men in oilskins were stationed at binocular,
And the horsemen by the river galloping anxiously this way and that
And the cry of hounds came tumbling invisibly with their echoes down through the draggle of trees,
Swinging across the wall of dark woodland,
The stag dropped in to strange country.

And turned at the river
Hearing the hound-pack smash the undergrowth, hearing the bell-note
Of the voice that carried all the others,
Then while his limbs all cried different directions to his lungs, which only wanted to rest,
The blue horsemen on the bank opposite
Pulled aside the camouflage of their terrible planet.

And the stag doubled back weeping and looking for home up a valley and down a valley
While the strange trees struck him and the brambles lashed him,
And the strange earth came galloping after him carrying the loll-tongued hounds to fling all over him
And his heart became just a club beating his ribs and his own hooves shouted with hounds' voices,
And the crowd on the road got back into their cars
Wet-through and disappeared.

Ted Hughes

Roe-Deer

In the dawn-dirty light, in the biggest snow of the year
Two blue-dark deer stood in the road, alerted.

They had happened into my dimension
The moment I was arriving just there.

They planted their two or three years of secret deerhood
Clear on my snow-screen vision of the abnormal

And hesitated in the all-way disintegration
And stared at me. And for some lasting seconds

I could think the deer were waiting for me
To remember the password and sign

That the curtain had blown aside for a moment
And there where the trees were no longer trees, nor the road a road

The deer had come for me.

Then they ducked through the hedge, and upright they rode their legs
Away downhill over a snow-lonely field

Towards tree dark – finally
Seeming to eddy and glide and fly away up

Into the boil of big flakes.
The snow took them and soon their nearby hoofprints as well

Revising its dawn inspiration
Back to the ordinary.

Ted Hughes

Iguana Memory

Saw an iguana once
when I was very small
in our backdam backyard
came rustling across my path

green like moving newleaf sunlight

big like big big lizard
with more legs than centipede
so it seemed to me
and it must have stopped a while
eyes meeting mine
iguana and child locked in a brief
split moment happening
before it went hurrying

for the green of its life

Grace Nichols

Keeping Orchids

The orchids my mother gave me when we first met
are still alive, twelve days later. Although

some of the buds remain closed as secrets.
Twice since I carried them back, like a baby in a shawl,

from her train station then mine, then home. Twice
since then the whole glass carafe has crashed

falling over, unprovoked, soaking my chest of drawers.
All the broken waters. I have rearranged

the upset orchids with troubled hands. Even after
that the closed ones did not open out. The skin

shut like an eye in the dark; the closed lid.
Twelve days later, my mother's hands are all I have.

Her face is fading fast. Even her voice rushes
through a tunnel the other way from home.

I close my eyes and try to remember exactly:
a paisley pattern scarf, a brooch, a navy coat.

A digital watch her daughter was wearing when she died.
Now they hang their heads,

and suddenly grow old – the proof of meeting. Still,
her hands, awkward and hard to hold

fold and unfold a green carrier bag as she tells
the story of her life. Compressed. Airtight.

A sad square, then a crumpled shape. A bag of tricks.
Her secret life – a hidden album, a box of love letters.

A door opens and closes. Time is outside waiting.
I catch the draught in my winter room.

Airlocks keep the cold air out.
Boiling water makes flowers live longer. So does

cutting the stems with a sharp knife.

Jackie Kay

Jackie Kay was adopted at birth and only found her birth mother in later life.

Mushrooms

Overnight, very
Whitely, discreetly,
Very quietly

Our toes, our noses
Take hold on the loam,
Acquire the air.

Nobody sees us,
Stops us, betrays us;
The small grains make room.

Soft fists insist on
Heaving the needles,
The leafy bedding,

Even the paving.
Our hammers, our rams,
Earless and eyeless,

Perfectly voiceless,
Widen the crannies,
Shoulder through holes. We

Diet on water,
On crumbs of shadow,
Bland-mannered, asking

Little or nothing.
So many of us!
So many of us!

We are shelves, we are
Tables, we are meek,
We are edible,

Nudgers and shovers
In spite of ourselves.
Our kind multiplies:

We shall by morning
Inherit the earth.
Our foot's in the door.

Sylvia Plath

The Flowers

After lunch my daughter picked
handfuls of the wild flowers
she knew her grandfather liked best
and piled them in the basket of her bicycle,
beside an empty jam-jar and a trowel;
then, swaying like a candle-bearer,
she rode off to the church
and, like a little dog, I followed her.

She cleared the grave of nettles
and wild parsley, and dug a shallow hole
to put the jam-jar in. She arranged
the flowers to look their best
and scraped the moss from the stone,
so you could see whose grave
she had been caring for.
It didn't take her long – no longer
than making his bed in the morning
when he had got too old to help her.

Not knowing how to leave him,
how to say good-bye, I hesitated
by the rounded grave. *Come on*,
my daughter said, *It's finished now*.
And so we got our bicycles and rode home
down the lane, moving apart
and coming together again,
in and out of the ruts.

Selima Hill

The Storm

1

Against the stone breakwater,
Only an ominous lapping,
While the wind whines overhead,
Coming down from the mountain,
Whistling between the arbors, the winding terraces;
A thin whine of wires, a rattling and flapping of leaves,
And the small street-lamp swinging and slamming against
the lamp pole.

Where have the people gone?
There is one light on the mountain.

2

Along the sea-wall, a steady sloshing of the swell,
The waves not yet high, but even,
Coming closer and closer upon each other;
A fine fume of rain driving in from the sea,
Riddling the sand, like a wide spray of buckshot,
The wind from the sea and the wind from the mountain contending,
Flicking the foam from the whitecaps straight upward into the darkness.

A time to go home!—
And a child's dirty shift billows upward out of an alley,
A cat runs from the wind as we do,
Between the whitening trees, up Santa Lucia,
Where the heavy door unlocks,
And our breath comes more easy—
Then a crack of thunder, and the black rain runs over us, over
The flat-roofed houses, coming down in gusts, beating
The walls, the slatted windows, driving
The last watcher indoors, moving the cardplayers closer
To their cards, their anisette.

3

We creep to our bed, and its straw mattress.
We wait; we listen.
The storm lulls off, then redoubles,
Bending the trees half-way down to the ground,
Shaking loose the last wizened oranges in the orchard,
Flattening the limber carnations.

A spider eases himself down from a swaying light-bulb,
Running over the coverlet, down under the iron bedstead.
Water roars into the cistern.

We lie closer on the gritty pillow,
Breathing heavily, hoping—
For the great last leap of the wave over the breakwater,
The flat boom on the beach of the towering sea-swell,
The sudden shudder as the jutting sea-cliff collapses,
And the hurricane drives the dead straw into the living pine-tree.

Theodore Roethke

Nettles

My son aged three fell in the nettle bed.
'Bed' seemed a curious name for those green spears,
That regiment of spite behind the shed:
It was no place for rest. With sobs and tears
The boy came seeking comfort and I saw
White blisters beaded on his tender skin.
We soothed him till his pain was not so raw.
At last he offered us a watery grin,
And then I took my billhook, honed the blade
And went outside and slashed in fury with it
Till not a nettle in that fierce parade
Stood upright any more. And then I lit
A funeral pyre to burn the fallen dead,
But in two weeks the busy sun and rain
Had called up tall recruits behind the shed:
My son would often feel sharp wounds again.

Vernon Scannell

Thistles

Against the rubber tongues of cows and the hoeing hands of men
Thistles spike the summer air
Or crackle open under a blue-black pressure.

Every one a revengeful burst
Of resurrection, a grasping fistful
Of splintered weapons and Icelandic frost thrust up

From the underground stain of a decayed Viking.
They are like pale hair and the gutturals of dialects.
Everyone manages a plume of blood.

Then they grow grey, like men.
Mown down, it is a feud. Their sons appear,
Stiff with weapons, fighting back over the same ground.

Ted Hughes

The Five Students

The sparrow dips in his wheel-rut bath,
The sun grows passionate-eyed,
And boils the dew to smoke by the paddock-path;
As strenuously we stride, –
Five of us; dark He, fair He, dark She, fair She, I,
All beating by.

The air is shaken, the high-road hot,
Shadowless swoons the day,
The greens are sobered and cattle at rest; but not
We on our urgent way, –
Four of us; fair She, dark She, fair He, I, are there,
But one – elsewhere.

Autumn moulds the hard fruit mellow,
And forward still we press
Through moors, briar-meshed plantations, clay-pits yellow,
As in the spring hours – yes,
Three of us; fair He, fair She, I, as heretofore,
But – fallen one more.

The leaf drops: earthworms draw it in
At night-time noiselessly,
The fingers of birch and beech are skeleton-thin,
And yet on the beat are we, –
Two of us; fair She, I. But no more left to go
The track we know.

Icicles tag the church-aisle leads,
The flag-rope gibbers hoarse,
The home-bound foot-folk wrap their snow-flaked heads,
Yet I still stalk the course –
One of us . . . Dark and fair He, dark and fair She, gone:
The rest – anon.

Thomas Hardy

A Blade of Grass

You ask for a poem.
I offer you a blade of grass.
You say it is not good enough.
You ask for a poem.

I say this blade of grass will do.
It has dressed itself in frost,
It is more immediate
Than any image of my making.

You say it is not a poem,
It is a blade of grass and grass
Is not quite good enough.
I offer you a blade of grass.

You are indignant.
You say it is too easy to offer grass.
It is absurd.
Anyone can offer a blade of grass.

You ask for a poem.
And so I write you a tragedy about
How a blade of grass
Becomes more and more difficult to offer,

And about how as you grow older
A blade of grass
Becomes more difficult to accept.

Brian Patten

Trout

Hangs, a fat gun-barrel,
deep under arched bridges
or slips like butter down
the throat of the river.

From depths smooth-skinned as plums
his muzzle gets bull's eye;
picks off grass-seed and moths
that vanish, torpedoed.

Where water unravels
over gravel-beds he
is fired from the shallows
white belly reporting

flat; darts like a tracer –
bullet back between stones
and is never burnt out.
A volley of cold blood

ramrodding the current.

Seamus Heaney

Break of Day in the Trenches

The darkness crumbles away—
It is the same old druid Time as ever.
Only a live thing leaps my hand—
A queer sardonic rat—
As I pull the parapet's poppy
To stick behind my ear.
Droll rat, they would shoot you if they knew
Your cosmopolitan sympathies.
Now you have touched this English hand
You will do the same to a German—
Soon, no doubt, if it be your pleasure
To cross the sleeping green between.
It seems you inwardly grin as you pass
Strong eyes, fine limbs, haughty athletes
Less chanced than you for life,
Bonds to the whims of murder,
Sprawled in the bowels of the earth,
The torn fields of France.
What do you see in our eyes
At the shrieking iron and flame
Hurled through still heavens?
What quaver—what heart aghast?
Poppies whose roots are in man's veins
Drop, and are ever dropping;
But mine in my ear is safe,
Just a little white with the dust.

Isaac Rosenberg

2 Non-fiction prose

From In The Empire Of Genghis Khan

Mongolian Wedding

Throughout the evening people came to warn me about themselves. They sat on the grass outside my tent, unburdening themselves with pre-emptive confessions. The following day would be difficult, they said. Weddings were boisterous occasions. People became unpredictable. They counselled me about particular individuals, then admitted that they themselves could be as bad as the next fellow. I would be wise to get away early before things got out of hand.

In the morning the groom and his supporters, a party of about seven or eight relations, set off to fetch the bride from her *ger*, which lay some 15 miles away. An old Russian truck, the equivalent of the wedding Rolls, had been specially hired for the occasion. When they arrived the groom would be obliged to search for his bride who by tradition must hide from him. It would not be too difficult. The tradition is that she hides under a bed in the neighbouring *ger*.

While we waited for their return we were given breakfast in the newlyweds' *ger*. Over the past weeks it had been lovingly prepared by relations. It was like a show *ger* from *Ideal Gers*. Decorations included a poster of the inspirational figure of Batardene, the national wrestling champion, which had been hung in a prominent position above the marital bed. Biscuits, slabs of white cheese and boiled sweets had been arrayed on every surface in dizzy tiers like wedding cakes. On a low stool stood a mountainous plate of sheep parts, with the favoured cut, the great fatty tail, like a grey glacier on its summit.

Younger sisters hustled in and out making last-minute preparations. While we were at breakfast the first lookouts were posted to watch for the return of the truck bearing the wedding party from the bride's camp.

By mid-afternoon we were still waiting. Apparently a wedding breakfast would have been given to the groom and his accompanying party at the bride's camp, and complicated calculations were now performed concerning the number of miles to the bride's *ger*, divided by the speed of the truck combined with the probable duration of the breakfast, and finally multiplied by the estimated consumption of *arkhi*.

At four o'clock a spiral of dust finally appeared beyond a distant ridge. When the truck drew up in front of the wedding *ger*, it was clear that the lavish hospitality of the bride's camp had been the cause of the delay. The back of the truck was crammed with wedding guests in such a state of dishevelled merriment that we had some difficulty persuading them to disembark. The bride's mother, apparently convinced that they were at the wrong *ger*, required four men to convey her to terra firma. The bride's elder sister, shrugging off all assistance, fell headfirst from the tailgate, bounced twice and came to rest, smiling, against a door post.

Once everyone was down from the truck, the bride and the groom stood respectfully to one side while the wedding party crowded into the new *ger*. The groom was tall and thin with a long, angular face. The bride, as round as he was linear, came up to his waist. Throughout the happy day they behaved like disappointed parties on a blind date, never once meeting each other's eyes.

Inside the newlyweds' *ger*, the two families took up positions on either side of the tent like opposing armies. Numbering 50 or 60 people, they were crowded together with the kind of intimacy usually reserved for the morning rush hour on the Tokyo subway.

The unexpected presence of a foreigner was seen as a sign of good fortune for the success of the union and I had been squeezed into the lap of one of the groom's brothers. At my back were the sharp knees of a long, disapproving line of grannies and elderly aunts seated on cots.

Mongolian weddings suffer from an excess of hospitality. After the morning's blowout at the bride's *ger*, it was now the turn of the groom's family to turn on the largesse, and they did not want to be outdone. Traditionally each guest had to drink three bowls of *airag* and three of *arkhi*. Younger sisters were deployed as cupbearers, picking their way through the crush of limbs as they ferried the bowls back and forth.

With the arrival of the third bowl of *airag* each guest was obliged to offer a song. For even the shyest Mongolians this was a fairly painless turn as the whole assembly knew all the songs by heart and joined in en masse before the end of the first line. Sadly they were less familiar with the Irish air *She Moves Through the Fair*, and I was obliged to sing all four verses, unaccompanied, to a silent and bemused audience.

It was only as I was coming to the end of the first verse that I remembered it was a song about a doomed wedding. Mongolians are very touchy about tempting fate and when they asked for a translation, I suggested to Mandah, my interpreter, that she should lie. She performed admirably, producing a story about a boy looking for his favourite horse.

The groom's brother, in his role as best man, was trying to bring some order to the proceedings, introducing members of the groom's family, welcoming the bride's family, directing the flow of *airag*. He wore the kind of peaked leather cap favoured by Lenin in the days when there was a revolution to lead. The resemblance was further underlined by a goatee and a tendency to stand and wave his arms about in declamatory fashion. He made several toasts. 'We will drink! We will feast! We will sing!' He made it sound like a Party directive.

One of the groom's brothers-in-law had taken a proprietorial interest in me. He wore a homburg and a red *del* and had the smile and face of a friendly small-town bank manager. He let it be known that he was helping to pay for the wedding.

He was a prosperous fellow with vast stocks of sheep. When it emerged that I was travelling by horse, he offered me his own horse, a priceless beast according to his own calculations. I demurred but he insisted. 'I'll kill a sheep tomorrow, you can take it with you,' he said. 'You are our guest. Whatever you need, food, horses, good luck, just let me know.' He held up his finger quizzically, 'Have you a wife?' he asked. 'Don't worry. We'll sort something out in the morning.'

On the other side of the *ger*, among the bride's family, the most prominent figures were her two brothers. The first, was a fine singer, who was much called upon during the afternoon for a song. The other brother could have played Wyatt Earp in a remake of *Gunfight at the OK Corral*. He had a broad-brimmed hat, a pencil moustache and handsome chiselled features. He had even mastered the cowboy trick of conveying an impression of intelligence and quiet dignity by never opening his mouth. When pressed for comment he invariably came up with the Mongolian equivalent of 'Yup'.

New reserves of *airag* were arriving. An elder sister of the bride arose at this point with a rather sarcastic vote of thanks followed by the announcement that the family were taking their leave. Apparently the feeling was that the groom's family were being rather too generous with the drink, and trying to belittle the bride's family by outdoing their hospitality of the morning. On cue, Wyatt Earp and the singer rose to depart, followed by the massed ranks of the bride's family. The groom's family, alarmed by this turn of events, sprang to their feet. 'You must stay,' they cried. 'Food is coming. There is more *airag*. You must enjoy yourselves.'

The groom's family pulled at the bride's family to keep them from departing, while the bride's family pulled strenuously towards the door. In no time the pulling, common to the friendliest of Mongolian drinking circles, had degenerated into a brawl. Someone had pulled too hard and toppled forward, flattening a granny. Someone else accidentally upset a bowl of *airag*.

Suddenly the *ger* was in uproar and blows were being exchanged. Wyatt Earp laid into a row of young men, felling three of them with a roundhouse right. The man in the homburg, smiling more widely than ever, floored the singer, sending the stove and an elderly aunt flying. Lenin tried to rescue the situation with one of his speeches. "We will drink! We will feast! We will sing!" he shouted above the mayhem. But no one was listening.

He chopped two of the bride's sisters to the ground and tried to push his way towards the door to block their escape route. One of the sharp-kneed aunts at my back had taken up a horsewhip and was merrily flailing in the direction of her new in-laws. Eight bowls of *airag* had not done much for her aim and the blows were raining down on my shoulders.

The bridal couple sat side by side, eyes politely downcast, as if the warfare that now raged about them was just another embarrassing speech. The only other non-participant was the *lama*, who viewed the fray with the eyes of a fight promoter while taking the opportunity of the general distraction to help himself to another bowl of *arkhi*.

The brawl came to an abrupt end with a strange good grace. It appeared fierce enough – there were at least a couple of bloody noses – but afterwards, with victory going to the groom's family for preventing what they saw as premature departure, everyone settled down to another round of drinking and songs. No one seemed to consider a wedding punch-up odd. With my own judgement slightly deranged by *airag*, I was happy to fall in with this consensus, and decided that this mixture of camaraderie and violence, with a few songs thrown in, was a rather healthy business. It cleared the air nicely. A wedding reception where you got to give your new in-laws a good thumping was the kind of thing that people in the West could only dream about.

Stanley Stewart

Glossary: *airag* – alcoholic liquor
arkhi – a clear spirit distilled from milk
del – article of clothing
ger – home
lama – priest
Wyatt Earp – legendary sheriff from the American Wild West era

From The Other Side of the Dale

There were only two classrooms: one for the infants and one for the juniors. Both were long square rooms with high beamed ceilings, both very bright and showing clear evidence of a range of high-quality work. In the infant classroom I met a small nervous-looking woman busy arranging a spray of flowers and ferns. She smiled weakly and introduced herself as Mrs Durdon, 'the teacher of the little ones'. Her hand trembled slightly and she blinked rapidly as she introduced herself.

In the junior classroom the small high-set windows had been removed and replaced by a large picture window which gave an uninterrupted and quite magnificent view across the moor and down into the valley.

From the classroom window, the cold bleak moor stretched before us, strange and desolate. A light grey mist hung low to the hard ground and the few dark skeletal trees, blackthorns and dwarf scrub, twisted skywards as if writhing in agony. No wind stirred, no birds sang. All was still and silent. It was a grim and gloomy picture but, at the same time, quite awesome.

'It's very beautiful in its own way, isn't it?' commented the Headteacher.

'It is,' I agreed. 'It must be fascinating to see how the seasons change from this classroom window.'

'Yes,' she sighed, 'we are very fortunate.' The noise of excited chatter outside interrupted our reverie. 'If you'll excuse me for a moment, Mr Phinn,' said Miss Precious, 'I can hear the first children arriving. Mrs Durdon and I like to welcome them each morning and say a few words to the parents.'

I was left alone and was still staring from the window when a small serious-faced boy with thick-lensed glasses like the bottoms of milk bottles entered and came across to me.

'Good morning,' he said. 'You must be the school inspector.'

'That's right,' I replied.

'Miss Precious said you would be coming today. Did you have a pleasant journey?'

'Yes, thank you.'

'We don't generally get visitors up here.'

'You are a bit out of the way, certainly.'

'I'm Joseph Richard Barclay.' He held out a small hand which I shook.

'And I'm Mr Phinn.'

'I'm pleased to meet you, Mr Phinn,' he said. 'Were you looking at the moor?'

'Yes. It really is a desolate scene. I don't think I've seen such a bleak and barren view quite like this one.'

'There was a famous battle there, you know, over four hundred years ago, between the Roundheads and the Cavaliers. A lot of men perished on that moor. They say the ground was red with blood.'

'Really?'

'It was called the Battle of Barton Moor but it was really only a skirmish. It wasn't your proper full-scale battle like Marston Moor or Naseby. The Cavaliers were pursued by the Roundheads up the valley but made a stand at Barton Moor. We sometimes get people visiting from the university.'

'You're quite the expert, aren't you, Joseph?'

The boy nodded seriously. 'I do like history. If you walk across the moor in the late afternoon, it's full of shadows and shapes and some say the ghosts of the dead soldiers wander about.'

I stared for a moment at my companion. He was a strangely old-fashioned looking boy of about eleven, with a curiously old-fashioned way of speaking. Eleven-year-olds generally do not use words like 'perished' and 'skirmish' and 'pursued'. His hair was of the short-back-and-sides variety, a style that I had sported when I had been his age and he wore long grey trousers, a hand-knitted grey pullover, long grey stockings and sensible shoes. He could have been a schoolboy of the 1950s. Miss Precious's precocious pupil, no doubt.

'Well,' he said suddenly, 'I must get on. I have to collect the register. If you'll excuse me.'

The school, which had been silent a few moments ago, was now full of business-like noise and bustle. One real pleasure in my job is to hear the animated conversations, lively exchanges and uninhibited laughter of young children as they arrive at school in the morning. Through the classroom door I heard a hubbub of excited children obviously clustering around their teachers as they hung up their coats and changed into their indoor shoes.

'Miss, t'watter in t'hen coops froz up last neight. It were as 'ard as Brimham Rocks.'

'T'calf were born last neight, miss – it's a really big 'un. Like a babby helephant, it were. I was up 'til ten with t'vet!'

'Miss, my mum says it's cold enough to freeze t'flippers off a penguin this mornin'.'

'Miss, did you see the heronsew on t'bank? Reight big 'un miss, looking for t'fish in t'stell.'

'Miss, t'pipes in our outside lavvy are frozzen solid. Mi dad couldn't oppen yat this morning, it were that stiff wi t'cold.'

I learnt later in the day that a 'heronsew' was a heron, a 'stell' a large open ditch and a 'yat' a gate. When the children caught sight of me, I was surrounded and treated to the same lively chatter, full of the richness of a Dales' dialect.

'Come on, come on, chatterboxes!' said Miss Precious, moving into the midst of the children like a great mother hen gathering up her chicks. 'You will have plenty of time to talk to Mr Phinn later this morning.' She turned in my direction. 'Could you start in Mrs Durdon's class with the infants, please, Mr Phinn, and join us after morning break?'

Mrs Durdon, despite her trembling and frequent blinking at the start of the lesson, proved to be a very good teacher and she soon relaxed after I have given her a few reassuring smiles and friendly nods. The classroom was neat and tidy and the children's work was well-displayed. A large bright alphabet and key words for children to learn decorated a wall and an attractive reading-corner contained a range of colourful picture and reading books and simple dictionaries. The standard of reading was high as was the quality of the written work.

A small rosy-faced child of about seven years old was busy tapping away at the computer in the corner, copying a piece of writing from her book. It was a delightful account and quite poetic in its use of language:

On Saturday we went for a pizza in Pickerton.
My brother Timmy had a pizza the size of his head.
He did not eat much because he sniffed some pepper up his nose.

He kept on sneezing and crying.
Mum was mad but my Dad laughed and laughed.
He said he would not do that in a hurry again.

At play-time Mrs Durdon donned a thick black coat, heavy scarf, white woolly hat and white boots and, explaining that she was on yard duty that morning, waddled off in the direction of the small playground. As I watched her, I recalled the comment I had heard earlier that morning: 'Miss, my mum says it's cold enough to freeze t'flippers off a penguin.'

A cup of coffee in a fine china cup was awaiting me in the Headteacher's room.

'Now,' she said taking two heavy, black leather-bound tomes from the shelf, 'I want you to have a look at the school log books. They are really fascinating and go back well over a century. We get all these visitors from the university to study the battlefield but these log books, Mr Phinn, contain much more interesting history in my opinion.'

She opened the first tome and passed it across her desk. The first page had the following entry:

September 5th, 1898
Took up my position as Headmaster of Barton Moor Parochial School in the County of York. 24 children on role, all from farming familys. Most of them iliterate.

'Isn't it just priceless,' chortled Miss Precious. 'Can you see how he's spelled "illiterate" and "families" and "roll" and it gets better.'

The next entry read:

September 6th 1898
Morning spent on arithmetic, handwriting and scripture. Afternoon spent on rhetoric. I learned them a poem.

'And they say standards have declined,' said Miss Precious. 'Now if you look at the page I've marked with a piece of paper, you will find the classic entry. It's the report of the school inspector.'

December 10th, 1913
The Inspector's Report to the School Board as follows: 'The affairs of this school are ill-managed by a committee of languid, inept amateurs and the school is staffed by two incompetent teachers. To form the minds of children and direct their efforts into beneficial channels, the teachers must at least know more than their charges. The Headmaster is so absorbed in administrative and financial concerns that he neglects the intellectual and spiritual development of the children.'

I looked up smiling. 'The inspectors could be pretty savage in those days, couldn't they?'

'Of course, the Headmaster was sacked,' continued Miss Precious. 'He seems to have just upped and gone following the inspector's visit. Just after the First World War the new Headmaster arrived, a Mr MacMillan. He is still remembered by some of the very old inhabitants in the village. He was known as Captain Mac, and was prone to ranting and raving and was a demon with the cane. Evidently he had seen action in the trenches and suffered terrible wounds, mental and physical, and wanted a quiet, untroubled life in Bartondale.' She flicked the pages. 'Captain Mac was a man of few words and stern disposition.'

The entries read:

Monday, December 9th
Heavy snow. Eight children absent. Direful day.

Tuesday, December 10th
More snow. Twelve children absent. Frozen pipes in boys' lavatory. Awful day.

Wednesday, December 11th
Still more snow. Only three children present. Frozen pipes in girls' lavatory. Appalling day.

Thursday, December 12th
Thaw sets in. Two absentees. School full of mud and water. Horrible day.

Friday, December 13th
Full complement of children. Burst pipes, flooded toilets. School inspector, Mr Thoroughgood, visited. Calamitous day!

'This is really interesting,' I said. 'Have you thought of writing a short history of the school and including all this material? It would make an excellent piece of action-research for the children.'

'We've done it,' she replied proudly. 'The children researched the history of Barton Moor Parochial School, collected photographs and old maps, made copies of parish records and interviewed parents and grandparents. We discovered a host of fascinating characters from the past: eccentric parsons, dyed-in-the wool farmers, hedgers and ditchers, colourful landlords of the local inn, a footpad who was hanged at York and the Lord of the Manor who ran off with a serving maid. We amassed great deal of information and Joseph put it all together. I think you met Joseph Barclay earlier this morning. He's the young man I wanted to pick your brains about. It was Joseph who produced a short but very readable account of the school's history.' She reached up and plucked a booklet from the shelf. The chronicle was word-processed in bold clear lettering and written in a style unusually mature for an eleven-year-old. It was illustrated by small line drawings, carefully executed maps and well mounted photographs.

'It's good, isn't it?' Miss Precious said. 'You'll see Joseph's other work next lesson. I would be very interested to know what you think of it and then I would really welcome some advice on his education. He's a very unusual little boy is Joseph Barclay, very unusual indeed.'

The very person we were talking about was in the classroom when I arrived at the end of morning break. He was busily tidying the books in the small corner library.

'Hello, Mr Phinn,' he said.

'Haven't you been out to play, Joseph?' I asked.

'No, sir. I had a few jobs to do in the classroom, I keep things ship-shape.'

'It's good to blow a few cobwebs away, you know, get a breath of fresh air, have a run around in the morning.'

'Oh, I get enough fresh air. I walk a mile to school each morning and a mile home in the afternoon. That keeps me hale and hearty.' I smiled at the old-fashioned turn of phrase.

When the children had settled at their desks after the morning break, Miss Precious began her lesson.

'Now children, she said, 'Emily's mother has been gardening again.' There was loud, good-humoured laughter and a few children groaned, 'Oh no!'

'And she found something.' Miss Precious turned to the corner of the classroom where I sat watching with interest. 'I should explain, Mr Phinn, that Emily, like most of the children in the class, lives close to Barton Moor and her garden goes right up to the site of the battlefield. Emily's mother has found some really interesting things in her garden, hasn't she, Emily?' A bright-faced little girl nodded. 'Tell us what your mother found yesterday.'

'Well,' began Emily, 'it's a sort of buckle. It's maybe from a belt or a bag. It's all rusted up but there is a little silver rose in the middle. My mum was pulling up some dead flowers and there it was.'

'We'll add that to our collection, shall we, Emily, and when someone comes up from the university in the better weather we can find out exactly what it is.'

'So other things have been found, have they?' I asked.

'Yes, sir,' announced a boy waving his hand and arm in the air as if hailing a taxi. 'My grandad found some lead musket balls and three brass buttons when he was mending a gate.'

'My dad found a sort of spear thing,' chimed in another. 'It was under the foundations when we built the extension. It's at the museum now. What was it called?' he said, turning to Joseph. 'You know that spear thing that my dad found. Can you remember what it was called?'

'It was a halberd,' replied Joseph, ' a sort of hatchet with a spike on the top which would have been mounted on a long wooden pole and used by the pikemen during the battle.'

'That's it!' shouted the boy. 'A halberd.'

'Has anyone else found anything in their gardens?' I asked.

'I found a dead cat, sir!' announced a large boy with a big placid face. This was received with some kindly laughter but I noticed that it failed to bring a smile to Joseph's lips. He sat sober-faced at the front desk like the receptionist at a funeral parlour.

'I don't think somehow that a dead cat, Ben,' chuckled the teacher, 'dates back to the Battle of Barton Moor. Soldiers were not in the habit of taking their pets into battle with them. I should think –'

'Excuse me, miss,' interrupted Joseph, 'some of the commanders did take their pets into battle with them. Prince Rupert had a dog – it was a toy poodle – called Boy, which he sat on his saddle and he took everywhere with him, even into the thick of the fighting.'

'Do you know, Mr Phinn,' said Miss Precious amiably, 'Joseph has more history in his little finger than I've got in my entire head.'

I spent the remainder of the morning listening to the children read confidently and clearly and examining their written work.

Gervase Phinn

From Writing Home

The Lady in the Van

In the 1970s, an eccentric lady who lived in an ancient van took up residence in Alan Bennett's road. Eventually, she moved herself and her van into his front garden.

The old van was towed away in April 1974 and another one provided by Lady W. ('a titled Catholic lady', as Miss S. always referred to her). Happy to run to a new (albeit old) van, Lady W. was understandably not anxious to have it parked outside her front door and eventually, and perhaps by now inevitably, the van and Miss S. ended up in my garden. This van was roadworthy, and Miss S. insisted on being the one to drive it through the gate into the garden, a manoeuvre which once again enabled her to go through her full repertoire of hand signals. Once the van was on site Miss S. applied the handbrake with such determination that, like Excalibur, it could never thereafter be released, rusting so firmly into place that when the van came to be moved ten years later it had to be hoisted over the wall by the council crane.

This van (and its successor, bought in 1983) now occupied a paved area between my front door and the garden gate, the bonnet of the van hard by my front step, its rear door, which Miss S. always used to get in and out of, a few feet from the gate. Callers at the house had to squeeze past the back of the van and come down the side, and while they waited for my door to be opened they would be scrutinized from behind the murky windscreen by Miss Shepherd. If they were unlucky, they would find the rear door open with Miss S. dangling her large white legs over the back. The interior of the van, a midden of old clothes, plastic bags and half-eaten food, was not easy to ignore, but should anyone Miss S. did not know venture to speak to her she would promptly tuck her legs back and wordlessly shut the door. For the first few years of her sojourn in the garden I would try and explain to mystified callers how this situation had arisen, but after a while I ceased to care, and when I didn't mention it nor did anyone else.

At night the impression was haunting. I had run a cable out from the house to give her light and heating, and through the ragged draperies that hung over the windows of the van a visitor would glimpse Miss S.'s spectral figure, often bent over in prayer or lying on her side like an effigy on a tomb, her face resting on one hand, listening to Radio 4. Did she hear any movements she would straightaway switch off the light and wait, like an animal that has been disturbed, until she was sure the coast was clear and could put the light on again. She retired early and would complain if anyone called or left late at night. On one occasion Coral Browne was coming away from the house with her husband, Vincent Price, and they were talking quietly. 'Pipe down,' snapped the voice from the van, 'I'm trying to sleep.' For someone who had brought terror to millions it was an unexpected taste of his own medicine.

December 1974. Miss S. has been explaining to me why the old Bedford (the van not the music-hall) ceased to go, 'possibly'. She had put in some of her home-made petrol, based on a recipe for petrol substitute she read about several years ago in a newspaper. 'It was a spoonful of petrol, a gallon of water and a pinch of something you could get in every High Street. Well, I got it into my head, I don't know why, that it was bicarbonate of soda, only I think I was mistaken. It must be either sodium chloride or sodium nitrate, only I've since been told sodium chloride is salt and the man in Boots wouldn't sell me the other, saying it might cause explosions. Though I think me being an older person he knew I would be more responsible. Though not all old ladies perhaps.'

February 1975. Miss S.'s daily emergence from the van was highly dramatic. Suddenly and without warning the rear door would be flung open to reveal the tattered draperies that masked the terrible interior. There was a pause, then through the veils would be hurled several bulging plastic sacks. Another pause, before slowly and with great caution one sturdy slippered leg came feeling for the floor before the other followed and one had the first sight of the day's wardrobe. Hats were always a feature: a black railwayman's hat with a long neb worn slightly on the skew so that she looked like a drunken signalman or a French guardsman of the 1880s; there was her Charlie Brown pitcher's hat; and in June 1977 an octagonal straw table mat, tied on with a chiffon scarf and a bit of cardboard for the peak. She also went in for green eyeshades. Her skirts had a telescopic appearance, as they had often been lengthened many times over by the simple expedient of sewing a strip of extra cloth around the hem, though with no attempt at matching. One skirt was made by sewing several orange dusters together. When she fell foul of authority she put it down to her clothes. Once, late at night, the police rang me from Tunbridge Wells. They had picked her up on the station, thinking her dress was a nightie. She was indignant. 'Does it look like a nightie? You see lots of people wearing dresses like this. I don't think this style can have got to Tunbridge Wells yet.'

Miss S. seldom wore stockings, and alternated between black pumps and brown carpet slippers. Her hand and feet were large, and she was what my grandmother would have called 'a big-boned woman'. She was middle-class and spoke in a middle-class way, though her querulous and often resentful demeanour tended to obscure this; it wasn't a gentle or a genteel voice. Running through her vocabulary was a streak of schoolgirl slang. She wouldn't say she was tired, she was 'all done up'; petrol was 'juice'; and if she wasn't keen on doing something she'd say 'I'm darned if I will.'

May 1976. I have had some manure delivered for the garden and, since the manure heap is not far from the van, Miss S. is concerned that people passing might think the smell is coming from there. She wants me to put a notice on the gate to the effect that the smell is the manure, not her. I say no, without adding, as I could, that the manure actually smells much nicer.

I am working in the garden when Miss B., the social worker, comes with a boxful of clothes. Miss S. is reluctant to open the van door, as she is listening to *Any Answers*, but eventually she slides on her bottom to the door of the van and examines the clothes. She is unimpressed.

MISS S.: I only asked for one coat.
MISS B.: Well, I brought three just in case you wanted a change.
MISS S.: I haven't got room for three. Besides, I was planning to wash this coat in the near future. That makes four.
MISS B.: This is my old nursing mac.
MISS S.: I have a mac. Besides, green doesn't suit me. Have you got the stick?
MISS B.: No. That's being sent down. It had to be made specially.
MISS S.: Will it be long enough?
MISS B.: Yes. It's a special stick.
MISS S.: I don't want a special stick. I want an ordinary stick. Only longer. Does it have a rubber thing on it?

When Miss B. has gone, Miss S. sits at the door of the van slowly turning over the contents of the box like a chimpanzee, sniffing them and holding them up and muttering to herself.

June 1976. I am sitting on the steps mending my bike when Miss S. emerges for her evening stroll. 'I went to Devon on Saturday,' she said. 'On this frisbee.' I suppose she means freebie, a countrywide concession to pensioners that BR ran last weekend. 'Dawlish I went to. People very nice. The man over the loudspeaker called us Ladies and Gentlemen, and so he should. There was one person shouted, only he wasn't one of us – the son of somebody, I think.' And almost for the first time ever she smiled, and said how they had all been bunched up trying to get into this one carriage, a great crowd, and how she had been hoisted up. 'It would have made a film,' she said. 'I thought of you.' And she stands there in her grimy raincoat, strands of lank grey hair escaping from under her headscarf. I am thankful people had been nice to her, and wonder what the carriage must have been like all that hot afternoon. She then tells me about a programme on Francis Thompson she'd heard on the wireless, how he had tried to become a priest but had felt he had failed in his vocation, and had become a tramp. Then, unusually, she told me a little of her own life, and how she tried to become a nun on two occasions, had undergone instruction as a novice, but was forced to give it up on account of ill-health, and that she had felt for many years that she had failed. But that this was wrong, and it was not a failure. 'If I could have had more modern clothes, longer sleep and better air, possibly, I would have made it.'

'A bit of a spree,' she called her trip to Dawlish. 'My spree.'

Alan Bennett

Glossary: *Vincent Price* – an actor famous for his roles in horror films

● Tuesday February 15 2000 *The Guardian*

Four hours from the summit of Everest, **Cathy O'Dowd** came across a stricken climber. She faced a brutal choice: to risk her own life in a doomed rescue – or to push on to the top. Here she explains why she left the barely breathing body

'Don't leave me here to die'

I stared at the body, blinking in disbelief. We were in the shadow of the First Step, so the light was dull. The body lay about 10 metres from where I stood and was angled away from me. It jerked – a horrible movement, like a puppet being pulled savagely by its strings.

We had been on a well-organised and, so far, successful trail towards the summit of Everest, worrying only about ourselves. Now a stranger lay across our path, moaning. Lhakpa shouted down at me and waved me to move on, to follow him up onto the Step. I looked back at the raggedly jerking figure.

Each team or solo climber did, or should, arrive at the mountain self-sufficient. Anyone who turned up assuming they could borrow food, clothing or tentage would receive short shrift. Similarly, you could not climb yourself to a standstill then expect other teams to risk their lives to save you.

Saving someone was not straight-forward. There was no emergency number to call, no mountain rescue to whom the problem could be handed over. We would not be able to walk away, feeling we had done our civic duty and that "the experts" were now in charge. Anyone who becomes immobile on a mountain as large and remote as Everest is probably going to die. On this side of the mountain, we would have to get the victim all the way back to base camp before we could contemplate trying to find a helicopter. If they had to be carried, that would require a number of teams, dozens of people, and at least three days climbing.

Whoever it was on the rocks in front of me was so badly incapacitated that they had spent the night out on the mountain rather than crawl down. Life lay in keeping moving, as that generated body heat and, with every metre of descent, moved you into thicker air. I suspected we had virtually no chance of saving this climber.

We stood to throw away an entire expedition: the money, the time, the thousands of vertical feet of physical and mental effort. We had sponsors who expected us to go for the summit. We had personal ambitions that pointed in the same direction. We were only 240 vertical metres from the top, only four or five hours in climbing time. We were so close to fulfilling everything we had set out to do.

Should we throw it all away for some rescue attempt that was doomed? The body was lying in a ghastly inverted V. It looked as if the climber's spine might be broken. If they couldn't walk they were probably condemned. Why waste time, stand around getting cold and demoralised, when the attempt was futile? Why not just turn away and climb on? This all ran through my head in the space of a few seconds. But all the debates, the issues, the logical analysis were useless. I simply could not do it. I could not put the summit of a mountain ahead of a human life. I would not want to live with myself if I could. However hopeless this person's situation might be, I had to try. I walked back to Ian, who was standing with Jangbu, watching Lhakpa climbing the First Step.

"That body's alive. I'm going to have a look." It took him a moment to understand what I was talking about. "We can't just leave," I insisted.

He nodded and I stepped down from the trail and walked across the loose shale towards the body. I thought it might be one of the Russian team. The person was lying with their harness clipped to a line of fixed rope, stomach uppermost, head and legs dangling down on either side. I knelt down cautiously next to the body and saw it was a woman.

"Don't leave me," she said. Her skin was milky white, and totally smooth. It was a sign of severe frostbite and it made her look like a porcelain doll. Her eyes stared up at me, unfocusing, pupils huge dark voids. "Don't leave me," she murmured again.

I felt sick. With her long, dark hair, she looked like me. For a shocked second, I felt as if I was glimpsing a possible future for myself. The fact that she was conscious both encouraged and appalled me. It might be possible to save her – or we might yet have to leave her.

"I need to fetch the rest of my team," I said to her. "We have several people here. We will try and help you. I will come back, I promise."

"Why are you doing this to me?" she asked.

Ian and Jangbu came back with me. Lhakpa, Pemba and Ci Luo, seeing the turn events had taken, began to descend towards us. The woman had no visible trauma injuries and her bizarre position turned out to be the result of complete muscular limpness. She was as helpless as a rag doll. It looked as if someone had clipped her harness to the end of a fixed rope, presumably so she would not slip down the slope, and had then left her to go for help. Next to her was an orange bottle of oxygen, of Russian make, and a mask. The bottle was empty.

While Ian and Jangbu pulled her straight, I collected her down gloves, which had been thrown to one side. Her jacket was over her shoulders but her arms were not in the sleeves. Our bodies can react bizarrely to trauma. A fairly common occurrence with severe hypothermia is a sensation of extreme warmth. The victim may start tearing off clothing; it looked as if she had done this.

The men tried to replace her clothing. Her hands were swollen masses, her arms limp. She had no motor control. As Ian tried to get her arms into her sleeves, she gave no resistance and no assistance. Jangbu was trying to give her hot juice from his thermos. Then they each grabbed her under one arm and tried to pull her into a sitting position against a boulder. She was a dead weight. The two strong men took several heaves to get her sitting, and then both doubled over, gasping for breath. It showed us what it would take to try to actually carry her anywhere, let alone carry her or drag her for days down the mountain.

We had no capacity for giving her oxygen. Her mask would not fit our bottles. We carried spare bottles but no spare masks. For the oxygen to have any effect, she would have to be put on high flow, and stay on for hours. A few whiffs would have no effect. One of us would have to go off oxygen permanently to give her a mask, which would exhaust our spare supplies very quickly. Until we established that we had a real chance of saving her, the risk was too great.

We had no means of communication with the outside world. Pemba tried calling base camp, but their set was not switched on.

"I am an American, I am an American," the climber suddenly said.

American? But the American team was below us, a full day behind. My mind wandered back to what I had seen the day before: two tiny figures at the foot of the First Step, one still, one moving around.

Could she be Fran, the bubbly American woman who had sat in our ABC kitchen tent one night, passing the hours while she waited for her husband, the Russian climber, Serguei? That might make sense. She and Serguei were climbing as a twosome. They had no Sherpas, no oxygen. They would not be in radio contact with others on the mountain. But that did not explain how she came to have an oxygen bottle lying next to her. Nor did it explain where he had gone. Three Uzbek climbers were approaching.

"Will you help us?" I asked. "This woman is dying. We might be able to carry her down. Would you help?"

The leader of the three looked down at me reluctantly. "We tried to help yesterday. We left her with oxygen. She is too far gone to help."

He spoke into his radio, presumably talking to his base camp. However, they did stay, watching Ian and Jangbu to see what decision they took. Ian had the climber by both shoulders and was speaking directly at her, his face only inches from hers. ""You have to help us. If you can help us, we can try and move you down the mountain. If you don't you are going to die." He was staring into her face, looking for some reaction. There was nothing. She knew we were there, but she was not mentally coherent. It was difficult to know what was left in her head.

I noticed her other crampon a few feet below us and took a tentative step down the slope to retrieve it, but immediately thought better of it. The slope was covered in loose rock shards, like a million smashed dinner plates. They were slipping away under my feet, rolling down the slope towards the Rongbuk Glacier 4,300 metres below us. It was like trying to move across ball-bearings. I could see how a climber, having lost their balance, would not be able to stop the downward momentum. Had that happened to Serguei?

Ian and Jangbu had been trying to pull the woman into an upright position. Ian thought that if she could take some of her weight on her feet, even if she could not actually walk, it might be possible to move her down the mountain with a climber at each shoulder. However, her legs simply crumpled under her weight, as useless as strands of spaghetti.

We had been with Fran for nearly an hour, standing still in temperatures of around -30°C. Perched perilously on the steep, unstable slope, I could not even stamp my feet for warmth. I was beginning to feel profoundly cold. My fingers were almost totally numb. I had full-body shivers and my teeth were chattering behind my oxygen mask.

The decision to leave Fran came upon us without much discussion. The Uzbek climbers and Lhakpa had long been of that opinion. What hope I had faded in the face of her incoherence, her physical incapacity. Now Ian and Jangbu straightened up and turned away. She had stopped talking and seemed to have sunk into unconsciousness. The thought of going on was intolerable. I had lost the will to reach the summit. Besides the physical drain of the cold, I was emotionally shattered. I had never encountered anything like this. I had passed bodies, I had had friends not come back, but I had never watched anyone die. Nor had I had to decide to leave them.

It was harder for me because she was female. It is not that I thought women immune to the risk, but it was such a male-dominated environment. Everywhere you turned, everyone you talked to was male. I climb because I enjoy it. I climb for the pleasure of the activity, of the surroundings. There was no pleasure left. I wanted to be down, to be off the mountain, to have both feet on flat ground.

After abandoning that attempt, O'Dowd went on, in 1999, to become the first woman to reach the summit from both south and north. Francys (Fran) Arsentiev died after O'Dowd's group left her. It later emerged that Fran had made it to the top, becoming the first American woman to do so without oxygen. Her husband Serguei also died on the mountain.

Cathy O'Dowd

This is an edited extract from *Just for the Love of It*, by Cathy O'Dowd, published by Free to Decide on March 2, £20.

Sport for All?

● Wednesday March 1 2000 *The Independent*

Save our children from the horrors of school sport

In anticipation of writing two simple words, I am already the victim of creeping anxiety. A film of sweat begins to coat my palms, my head is swimming with visions of ogre-like teachers and I feel a deep sense of shame. Anyway: forward rolls ... there, I've done it.

When I was six or thereabouts, my inability to move myself a couple of feet, via the strange expedient of turning my body through 360 degrees, was a major source of trauma. My teachers quite reasonably believed that such a handicap would turn me into an unemployed vagrant, so I was forced to spend several months correcting it.

Just short of my seventh birthday, I cracked it. I now proudly include the ability to do forward rolls on my curriculum vitae.

These days, primary school pupils might be avoiding such nonsense. According to a survey released yesterday by the official development organisation Sport England, only 11 per cent of children aged six to eight spent two hours or more a week in PE lessons last year, down almost a third on 1995.

In response to this news, a parade of concerned sporting figures waffled on about the necessity of 'instilling' sport in kids from a young age, and how, without compulsory gymnastics, rugby and the Eton Wall Game, our success on the international stage will continue to decline. PE, we were told, is all that stands between lardy failure and the triumph of finely-toned Gods.

But the causal link that allegedly lies between national glory and damp mornings spent responding to the yelps of borderline psychopaths is cloudy indeed. Upon my arrival at secondary school, it became clear that forward rolls were only the start of my woes. When you're standing against a wall, roundly humiliated by being picked last for football once again, it's difficult to conclude that your misery is an integral part of a process that will result in Olympic Gold, world records, and the England Soccer team avoiding yet another early flight home.

In fact, the tradition of making sport synonymous with such treats as public embarrassment and being forced to act against one's will tended to put off even the people who were good at it.

The behaviour of some games teachers hardly helped matters. I recalled one prodigiously talented young athlete being slammed against a brick wall for expressing his reluctance to attend yet another Saturday morning cross-country meeting. It did not take long before he had thrown away his singlet and joined our gang. Long since resigned to sporting ineptitude, we had taken the shining path to a thrice-daily smoke behind the biology block. He happily joined in. One more convert to Embassy Filter, one lost medal for the UK.

At around 15, when school rules suddenly looked less scary, we aesthetes suddenly found a way to turn compulsory games into something bordering on performance art. We called it 'Team For A Laugh'. You cajoled one of the captains into picking all the people who were useless, and then attempted to rack up the most resounding defeat. Those who were potential sporting stars were livid – but if we were going to be press-ganged into sharing their pitch, this was the price we exacted.

In ever-sensible Germany, thanks to the very Teutonic idea of the pursuit of excellence, sport has long been an optional part of school life. Much like the orchestra, the art club and perfecting one's skill at chess, the Germans place sport in that box marked 'pastimes best enjoyed by those who are good at them'.

If Trevor Brooking, Chairman of Sport England, and others are to be believed, that makes them a fat, useless nation who are bad at everything. Erm, not sure about that one, Trev.

John Harris

● Tuesday March 27 2001 *Washington DC dispatch, The Guardian*

The godlike status afforded to student athletes in America has left the so-called 'nerds' and 'dweebs' feeling isolated and angry, writes Julian Borger

School sports culture leads to violence

One of the highlights of the US sporting year is approaching its climax. It is known as 'March Madness' – and with good reason. It pits basketball teams from across the country against each other in a knockout tournament that is watched by tens of thousands of fans in huge sporting arenas and by tens of millions on television.

It is huge business, and the most extraordinary thing about it is that the players are all college students. The idea takes a little getting used to for an outsider.

I played some football (soccer in US terms) at university in Britain, and our maximum crowd numbered about a dozen. Even the good college teams would have near fainted at the idea of being on television.

The only college sports event with a mass audience is the annual Oxford – Cambridge boat race, and that owes much of its popularity to a national fondness for tradition.

The transatlantic difference is even more striking on the secondary school level. In small town America, whole communities regularly turn out to watch the high-school team play baseball, or American football or basketball.

Schoolchildren can be heroes for the day. It is an all-encompassing social event of a kind rarely witnessed any more in English towns, and it is one where the focus of attention is exclusively on young people.

Nor is this school-age sporting culture confined to boys. Due to a piece of legislation called Title IX, passed in 1972, girls are guaranteed equal spending and support in school sport, and parents appear to pay the game just as much respect. Girls' football (soccer) is even bigger than the boys' version, helped by the fact that the women's team won the last World Cup.

The downside to this phenomenon, however, is obvious and it is beginning to take its toll. If children who are good at sports are heroes, what does that make those who are not?

Underlying the recent spate of school shootings have been stories of bullying and exclusion of non-athletes by the school 'jocks'.

After a frustrated schoolboy shot two other students dead earlier this month in the Californian town of Santee, an entire subculture of bullying came to the surface.

An angry young reader wrote to the Los Angeles Times: "For school personnel to be at a loss as to the motives of the shootings at Santana High School is hypocritical. Anyone who has attended high school knows there is the 'in crowd' made up of sports heroes, class officers and their entourage.

"To this group the teachers and administrators pander, allowing them to do pretty much as they please. Those not in the 'in group' become the subjects of bullying, taunting and ridicule. They are the nerds, dweebs etc."

The relentless rise of college sports has taken its toll in other ways. Many of the colleges have become addicted to the millions that their sports teams bring in, in the form of commercial sponsorship and ticket sales.

Increasingly they go out in search of young talents who have not finished secondary school. The academic role of these underage prodigies is often a polite pretence. In many of the big basketball playing colleges, the graduation rate among the players is well under 50%.

The term 'student-athlete' rings hollow in what has largely become a training ground for the professional league, the NBA, and those who do not make the transition often end up with nothing to show for their years in college.

It is a high risk for a fleeting chance at stardom. It would have been nice to have a few more people turn up to watch us play football in our college days, but the most casual glance through the US daily press demonstrates there is a price to be paid for taking student sports too seriously.

Julian Borger

• Tuesday August 14 2001 *The Guardian*

Does physical activity help to build not only a better body but a better brain? Wendy Berliner on an exercise with great promise for government ambitions on both sport and academic levels

Mind games

The summer holidays are in full swing. Inside thousands of homes, children slump on the couch watching television and playing computer games, curtains closed to stop the sunshine hitting the screen and spoiling the images.

Some of them will go swimming, play tennis, or get on their bikes, but a lot won't. Health experts agonise about the damage the couch potato kids are doing to their systems, but a growing body of evidence seems to suggest that, in the short term at least, their academic performance might be more affected by their sedentary life styles.

Research is still in its infancy, but the argument goes basically like this: increased physical activity increases blood flow to the brain and, when coupled with learning tasks (physical or mental), causes the formation of dendrites – the slender filaments that branch out of the neurons and increase the neural pathways and neural mapping of the brain. This is believed to increase intelligence in mammals and foster greater learning through improved intelligence.

Susan Greenfield, professor of pharmacology at Oxford University and one of the world's leading experts on the brain, says that your activities do affect the brain. US studies have shown that, for example, listening to classical music can raise the IQ and that, in later age, slumping on a couch to watch TV may cause Alzheimer's. "The brain is very sensitive to what is happening to the body and the more you are interacting and stimulating the circuits of the brain, the more agile are your brain cells," says Greenfield.

In Exeter, a project called Fit to Succeed – in which children at seven middle schools were encouraged to take part in much more regular physical activity – appears to be proving the link with academic performance. Scores in government SATS tests have been highest in the children who reported exercising at least three times a week. And it hasn't been just children from middle-class homes, who might have had more opportunity for extra activities, who have been getting better marks. The effect is clearly discernible in children on free school meals – those from economically disadvantaged homes. If they are exercising at least three times a week, they are getting better SATS scores.

Steve Kibble, senior physical education adviser for Devon, says: "More active children are more alert. After exercise the metabolism is raised for four or five hours – medical evidence supports this. We can't say physical activity will improve your IQ, but it does help maximise learning potential. We should be looking much more holistically at education. What point is there having five A-levels if you are going to die at 26 from cardiovascular problems?"

Research in different parts of the world points to a link between levels of activity and improvements in learning potential. In a long-term French study, pupils had their normal timetable modified throughout the final year of their primary education. The school week was lengthened by 9.5 hours, and two siestas were introduced each day. Academic instruction was curtailed by 26% and was limited to mornings. The afternoons were occupied by a wide range of physical activities such as gymnastics, swimming and sport. The progress of the experimental group was then compared with that of students attending other schools in the Paris area.

The fascinating finding was that although the extra activity group was getting 26% less lesson time, the proportion failing to attain the 'certificate of study' for the end of their primary education was no worse than the other students. Pupils were also more calm and attentive, and exhibited fewer disciplinary problems.

Ben Tan, director of the British Heart Foundation's national centre for physical activity and health at Loughborough University, has reviewed much research and says: "There does seem to be a strong correlation between high levels of physical activity and high academic achievement in schools. It increases the concentration of children and their ability to learn. In schools that invest in PE and after-school sport you can see a major improvement in academic achievement.

This is borne out by the early results of a three-year investigation into the effectiveness of physical education and school sport begun in April last year by the Qualifications and Curriculum Authority. QCA researchers conducted in-depth interviews at 30 schools and found that those with high participation in sports tend to have lower truancy rates and less bad behaviour. Regular and frequent participation in purposeful physical activity, they say, enables young people to significantly improve their physical competence, confidence and levels of attainment, health, fitness, well-being, self-esteem, motivation and, crucially, their attitudes to, and engagement in, learning.

continued

School sport and PE have been squeezed and neglected in recent years by government emphasis on improving academic standards. And tight local authority budgets have seen school sports fields being sold off.

According to research by Sport England published last year, the amount of sport played in primary schools had been reduced by a third in the previous five years. Those children and teenagers idling their summers away in front of computer and TV screens are the product of a school system which has advanced improvements in academic performance at the expense of physical activity.

If they had kept up the levels of physical activity of previous school generations, they might also have been achieving the higher levels of academic performance the government was looking for all along.

Wendy Berliner

● Monday October 8 2001 *Greenock Telegraph*

Report to the people

Sport in Schools

I have long thought that our aversion to exercise in Scotland may come from unpleasant memories of school sports.

As far as I remember, my experience of physical 'education' in school consisted of running up muddy hills; swimming past the icebergs in the Battery Park as the technical teacher had a fag – pausing briefly to shout that we weren't drowning and if we didn't shut up he *would* give us hypothermia; and being forced to play something called rugby.

But PE in schools wasn't as important then.

We got plenty of exercise away from school, chasing buses, sugar lorries, ice cream vans and milk motors. We also used to play street games – from enduring favourites such as football and rounders, to those which have not stood the test of time, such as ring, bang, skoosh and Cowboys and Indians.

And even watching television kept us fit. We lived in the bottom flat, with our TV aerial in the tenement loft. Every time we lost the picture, I was dispatched up four floors to hang from the skylight, performing gymnastics in attempt to get *Joe 90* in focus.

But how times have changed.

Children are more likely to be managing Brazil on their Playstation than kicking a ball outside in the street. They are more used to being driven to school in the family car, than running for a bus. It is more common for a child today to learn about brain trauma from the kids' science channel, than it is for them to enter a boxing ring.

So, if today's young people aren't getting exercise in their spare time, the quality of PE in schools becomes far more important.

It was good to see last week, then, the Scottish Parliament debating how we improve sport and make the most of the positive advantages it offers. Time and again, MSPs underlined how crucial sport is, not only in keeping children fit, healthy and away from cigarettes and drugs, but in giving them discipline and self-confidence.

That is why there is a raft of measures being undertaken at every level – school, local authority and national – to encourage children to get involved in sport at school.

The health benefits are clear. The social benefits are clear. And, with a spot of luck, the benefits to our national teams could be just around the corner.

Duncan McNeil, MSP
(Member of Scottish Parliament)

Parents and Children

● THE TIMES SATURDAY APRIL 3 1999

Parents learn how to say NO

Liberal generation discovers discipline

A generation of parents raised according to the permissive gospels of postwar childcare gurus is rediscovering the importance of saying 'No' to its children.

The word 'discipline', which had virtually disappeared from childcare manuals of the past two decades, is reappearing in family magazines and a stream of best selling 'how to' parenting manuals.

Parents who had retreated behind study doors to escape their overbearing, whingeing children are beginning to reclaim the house as their own. Even smacking is back on the agenda.

Parent Network, which runs 250 parenting courses throughout Britain, reports a growing demand for advice on how to control their children from parents who were brought up according to the liberal theories of experts such as the American Benjamin Spock.

While today's parents do not want to return to the harshness of the Victorian era – when children were seen, smacked, but not heard – there is a growing acknowledgement that the *laisser-faire* approach to childrearing went too far. It produced a generation of too many spoilt brats running rings around bemused parents struggling to restore order.

Janthea Brigden, a trainer with Parent Network, says: "The problem is that parents don't want all that controlling stuff that came with old fashioned discipline. What they want is to be able to discipline their children through teaching them and encouraging them." Steve Biddulph, a psychologist and author of *More Secrets of Happy Children*, believes that the permissive era was often just an excuse to ignore children, as adults were "just too busy being groovy". The alternative approach of teaching children how to get things right does take time, but pays off.

Mr Biddulph has taught discipline skills to more than 3,000 parents in countries from Spain to China, Germany to Scotland. He believes that discipline means teaching, and does not need to involve punishment. "Time-out – the usual fallback of psychologists – is a good emergency measure, but it doesn't teach a child anything."

According to Mr Biddulph, discipline usually involves firm but friendly confrontations. He teaches a method called 'stand and think', where a child is helped to figure out what it is doing wrong and how to get it right. It is a method he has also used with police and government agencies that need to re-educate difficult staff. Although he understands parents using smacking, he says he is against it, adding that 70 per cent of parents who hit their children also hit their spouses.

But giving up smacking does not mean letting children run amok. "The happiest children are those who know mum and dad are in charge. They can count on fairness, and consideration, but, when it comes to the crunch, what mum and dad says goes."

As children grow into their teens, more negotiation can take place, such as "Prove you can be home safely by 11pm, and we might let you stay out till midnight."

Alexandra Frean, Social Affairs Correspondent

● Thursday April 13 2000 *The Independent*

Pay your children too much attention and you could do more harm than good

Professional parents who are anxious to give their child the best start in life by 'hot-housing' them with educational toys, focused play and constant attention in the limited time they have available could be doing more harm than good, an expert said yesterday.

Matthew Melmed, chief executive of Zero to Three, a charity dedicated to the healthy development of infants, told a conference on parenting that children who were overstimulated when they were young were less curious, competent and able to deal with the outside world in later life.

Other research, reported in yesterday's *Independent*, has indicated that children whose parents did not turn off the television or radio when they talked to them at eight months old were at risk of becoming future criminals.

There has been much controversy in Britain about the benefits of 'hot-housing'. Many parents have turned to educational play to improve their children's verbal and cognitive skills to ensure they are accepted by good schools.

A survey by Zero to Three found that 87 per cent of parents believed the more stimulation a baby received the better. Mr Melmed said: "This finding is of particular concern given the attention on early brain development. It may make some parents feel driven to do more to 'stimulate' their baby's brain. The downside is that some parents will push toddlers and babies much further than they are developmentally capable of going, often to the child's long-term detriment.

"This very parent-directed interaction can lower children's curiosity, competence and ability to deal with the world on their own terms," he told the Parent Child 2000 conference in London organised by the National Family and Parenting Institute.

Spending 'quality time' with your child is not needed either, he said, as children benefit more from 'unhurried time' even if the parent is doing household chores.

Elizabeth Howell, of the Parenting Connections consultancy, said overstimulation was a form of child abuse. "Children who are bombarded with stimuli become overwhelmed and they shut down," she said.

Cherry Norton, Social Affairs Editor

● Friday September 7 2001 *The Guardian*

Use persuasion not coercion

First, let me make it very clear: I hate violence against children. I have never smacked my own children and never would. When I have witnessed other parents smacking their children, I have been horrified – it never seemed appropriate and it always struck me as an example of a parent with a lousy temper out of control.

But nor do I like parents shouting at their children or even the way parents can cajole and manipulate them to suit their own ends. "Oooh sweetie, you don't want to come with mummy, you stay here with the babysitter". Sounds innocuous? Of course, but you are basically telling your child that they don't know what they want. Do that often enough and the child will cease really knowing what he or she wants.

The point is that there is a whole range of parental behaviour towards children which is detrimental to their wellbeing and about which the state cannot do anything. There is a fine line to tread here between the state's duty to protect the rights of the child and its duty to respect the family's right to privacy, and the Scottish executive's proposal to ban smacking children under three has bulldozed through that line.

To pass a law against smacking toddlers is a ludicrous intervention into one of the most intimate and private relationships. Laws already exist to protect children from child abuse – the courts can judge already what constitutes 'unreasonable force'. The new proposals are about criminalising even the smack on the leg to which most parents admit they sometimes, in sheer frustration, resort.

Parenting is a 24/7 task, quite unlike any other form of childcare in its intensity and relentlessness. Teachers and nursery assistants are rightly banned from using corporal punishment. But parents are a different case; even the best of good parents sometimes snap – should that be made a crime? All parents know that they sometimes fail and that can haunt the anxious – does the exhausted mother dealing with a toddler tantrum at the checkout as well perhaps as a wailing baby now have to worry whether the checkout girl will report her to the police if she smacks her child?

By all means campaign against parents resorting to a smack, run parenting classes and so on, but the law is simply too crude a weapon to use in such circumstances. Persuasion not coercion is the way to achieve this cultural change. Besides, the law is simply unenforceable – who can see into the privacy of the family home? – as even the campaigners in support of the measure seem to accept when they talk about 'using the law to send clear messages'. But that is not what the law is there for. You use modern communications to send clear messages and you use the law to enforce and to punish crimes. The mother or father who slaps needs help, they do not need to be turned into criminals.

Madeleine Bunting

● June 19 2001 *Children's Express*

Smacking not the answer, say kids

By European standards the United Kingdom lags behind on the issue of children's rights, particularly regarding the use of physical punishment. Later this year, young people and adults will be asked for their views on smacking as the European Court of Justice attempts to clarify what is meant in legal terms by reasonable chastisement.

"Wait till I get you home, then I will give you something to cry about," screams an angry parent at her red-faced five-year-old son, who bawls as he is dragged through the supermarket aisles nursing a throbbing clipped ear.

Was it right of the adult to lash out at the child? Did the child deserve what he got? Should all forms of physical punishment be banned?

"I don't think it is good to hit your child, especially in public. Just think of the embarrassment and pain your child is going through when you hurt them in front of everyone," said Paul McAteer, 13.

Memories of being hit by a parent can stand out more than any other single event for many teenagers like Paul.

"I was kicking a ball in the entry against the wall at my granny's, I was told not to and stopped for about two seconds, then I came back and started again. One of my relatives called me in and hit me. That happened a long time ago but I still feel an emotional scar," he said.

Children are Unbeatable, an alliance of children's organisations, is spearheading a campaign in Northern Ireland to prevent the use of physical punishment.

They aim to change the law and ensure children have the same rights as adults when it comes to physical assault. Just under a third of Northern Ireland's population are children.

"Parents should find other means of discipline instead of smacking, which is basically hurting your own child and it is sort of barbaric when you think about it," said Hugo McIlveen, 15.

"I think parents should take away their children's privileges. If parents stop your allowance and you can't go out with your mates, you will seriously think twice before doing something wrong again," he added.

Like many other young people, Sheena Hall, 14, thinks smacking does not stop bad behaviour and sends out a negative message. "Smacking is not a good way of discipline because it is saying that physical violence is OK."

"Some parents are so stressed out that they build everything up inside them and then use their children as punchbags – they need to stop doing that and get help instead of taking it out on their children," she added.

Some parents don't think of smacking or a clip around the ear as 'real' physical punishment; others think disciplining their children is a private matter and no-one else's business, certainly not the government's.

"If there was a ban on smacking, it might reduce the amount of smacking going on at home but it would never completely stop it," said Christopher McCartney, 15.

"It distances you from your parents if they hit you. You don't want to talk to them about anything," Christopher added.

Colin Reid, Policy Adviser at NSPCC, which supports a legal ban on smacking, says adults' attitudes need to change.

"For some children smacking does not work and we need to move to a culture that uses other forms of discipline which promote positive outcomes for parents and children," he said.

Twenty years ago, Sweden banned the smacking of children. There has been overwhelming support for the ban and a marked reduction in serious child abuse cases.

Thomas Kielty, 15, said that relationships can become very strained if there is a threat of physical discipline.

"You would start lying to your parents if you thought it would get you out of trouble and avoid getting a smacking," he said.

Chris King, 15, thinks smacking is acceptable sometimes. "You should try everything else first, grounding or taking their money away. If that does not work the only way left is to hit them but you should not hit them hard, just enough to make them realise that they should stop what they are doing."

This article was produced by Andrew Bailie, 13, Sheena Hall, 14, Amanda McAteer, 13, Paul McAteer, 14, and Lucas Dillon, 10. It was published in *The News Letter* in Northern Ireland.

3 Different Cultures and Traditions

Short Stories

Country Lovers

The farm children play together when they are small; but once the white children go away to school they soon don't play together any more, even in the holidays. Although most of the black children get some sort of schooling, they drop every year farther behind the grades passed by the white children; the childish vocabulary, the child's exploration of the adventurous possibilities of dam, *koppies*, *mealie lands* and *veld* – there comes a time when the white children have surpassed these with the vocabulary of boarding-school and the possibilities of inter-school sports matches and the kind of adventures seen at the cinema. This usefully coincides with the age of twelve or thirteen; so that by the time early adolescence is reached, the black children are making, along with the bodily changes common to all, an easy transition to adult forms of address, beginning to call their old playmates *missus* and *baasie* – little master.

The trouble was Paulus Eysendyck did not seem to realize that Thebedi was now simply one of the crowd of farm children down at the *kraal*, recognizable in his sisters' old clothes. The first Christmas holidays after he had gone to boarding-school he brought home for Thebedi a painted box he had made in his wood-work class. He had to give it to her secretly because he had nothing for the other children at the kraal. And she gave him, before he went back to school, a bracelet she had made of thin brass wire and the grey-and-white beans of the castor-oil crop his father cultivated. (When they used to play together, she was the one who had taught Paulus how to make clay oxen for their toy *spans*.) There was a craze, even in the *platteland* towns like the one where he was at school, for boys to wear elephant-hair and other bracelets beside their watch-straps; his was admired, friends asked him to get similar ones for them. He said the natives made them on his father's farm and he would try.

When he was fifteen, six feet tall, and tramping round at school dances with the girls from the 'sister' school in the same town; when he had learnt how to tease and flirt and fondle quite intimately these girls who were the daughters of prosperous farmers like his father; when he had even met one who, at a wedding he had attended with his parents on a nearby farm, had let him do with her in a locked storeroom what people did when they made love – when he was as far from his childhood as all this, he still brought home from a shop in town a red plastic belt and gilt hoop ear-rings for the black girl, Thebedi. She told her father the missus had given these to her as a reward for some work she had done – it was true she sometimes was called to help out in the farmhouse. She told the girls in the kraal that she had another sweetheart nobody knew about, far away, away on another farm, and they giggled and teased, and admired her. There was a boy in the kraal called Njabulo who said he wished he could have bought her a belt and ear-rings.

When the farmer's son was home for the holidays she wandered far from the kraal and her companions. He went for walks alone. They had not arranged this; it was an urge each followed independently. He knew it was she, from a long way off. She knew that his dog would not bark at her. Down at the dried-up river-bed where five or six years ago the children had caught a leguaan one great day – a creature that combined ideally the size and ferocious aspect of the crocodile with the harmlessness of the lizard – they squatted side by side on the earth bank. He told her traveller's tales: about school, about the punishments at school, particularly, exaggerating both their nature and his indifference to

them. He told her about the town of Middleburg, which she had never seen. She had nothing to tell but she prompted with many questions, like any good listener. While he talked he twisted and tugged at the roots of white stinkwood and Cape willow trees that looped out of the eroded earth around them. It had always been a good spot for children's games, down there hidden by the mesh of old, ant-eaten trees held in place by vigorous ones, wild asparagus brushing up between the trunks, and here and there prickly-pear cactus sunken-skinned and bristly, like an old man's face, keeping alive sapless until the next rainy season. She punctured the dry hide of a prickly-pear again and again with a sharp stick while she listened. She laughed a lot at what he told her, sometimes dropping her face on her knees, sharing amusement with the cool shady earth beneath her bare feet. She put on her pair of shoes – white sandals, thickly Blanco-ed against the farm dust – when he was on the farm, but these were taken off and laid aside, at the river-bed.

One summer afternoon when there was water flowing there and it was very hot she waded in as they used to do when they were children, her dress bunched modestly and tucked into the legs of her pants. The schoolgirls he went swimming with at dams or pools on neighbouring farms wore bikinis but the sight of their dazzling bellies and thighs in the sunlight had never made him feel what he felt now, when the girl came up the bank and sat beside him, the drops of water beading off her dark legs the only points of light in the earth-smelling, deep shade. They were not afraid of one another, they had known one another always; he did with her what he had done that time in the storeroom at the wedding, and this time it was so lovely, so lovely he was surprised . . . and she was surprised by it, too – he could see in her dark face that was part of the shade, with her big dark eyes, shiny as soft water, watching him attentively: as she had when they used to huddle over their teams of mud oxen, as she had when he told her about detention weekends at school.

They went to the river-bed often through those summer holidays. They met just before the light went, as it does quite quickly, and each returned home with the dark – she to her mother's hut, he to the farmhouse – in time for the evening meal. He did not tell her about school or town any more. She did not ask questions any longer. He told her, each time, when they would meet again. Once or twice it was very early in the morning; the lowing of the cows being driven to graze came to them where they lay, dividing them with unspoken recognition of the sound read in their two pairs of eyes, opening so close to each other.

He was a popular boy at school. He was in the second, then the first soccer team. The head girl of the 'sister' school was said to have a crush on him; he didn't particularly like her, but there was a pretty blonde who put up her long hair into a kind of doughnut with a black ribbon round it, whom he took to see films when the schoolboys and girls had a free Saturday afternoon. He had been driving tractors and other farm vehicles since he was ten years old, and as soon as he was eighteen he got a driver's licence and in the holidays, this last year of his school life, he took neighbours' daughters to dances and to the drive-in cinema that had just opened twenty kilometres from the farm. His sisters were married, by then; his parents often left him in charge of the farm over the weekend while they visited the young wives and grandchildren.

When Thebedi saw the farmer and his wife drive away on a Saturday afternoon, the boot of their Mercedes filled with fresh-killed poultry and vegetables from the garden that it was part of her father's work to tend, she knew that she must come not to the river-bed but up to the house. The house was an old one, thick-walled, dark against the heat. The kitchen was its lively thoroughfare, with servants, food supplies, begging cats and dogs, pots boiling over, washing being damped for ironing, and the big deep-freeze the missus had ordered from town, bearing a crocheted mat and a vase of plastic irises. But the dining-room with the bulging-legged heavy table was shut up in its rich, old smell of soup and tomato sauce. The sitting-room curtains were drawn and the TV set silent. The door of the parents' bedroom was locked and the empty rooms where the girls had slept had sheets of plastic spread over the beds. It was in one of these that she and the farmer's son stayed together whole nights – almost: she had to get away before the house servants, who knew her, came in at dawn. There was a risk someone would discover her or traces of her presence if he took her to his own bedroom, although she had looked into it many times when she was helping out in the house and knew well, there, the row of silver cups he had won at school.

When she was eighteen and the farmer's son nineteen and working with his father on the farm before entering a veterinary college, the young man Njabulo asked her father for her. Njabulo's parents met with hers and the money he was to pay in place of the cows it is customary to give a prospective bride's parents was settled upon. He had no cows to offer; he was a labourer on the Eysendyck farm, like her father. A bright youngster; old Eysendyck had taught him brick-laying and was using him for odd jobs in construction, around the place. She did not tell the farmer's son that her parents had arranged for her to marry. She did not tell him, either, before he left for his first term at the veterinary college, that she thought she was going to have a baby. Two months after her marriage to Njabulo, she gave birth to a daughter. There was no disgrace in that; among her people it is customary for a young man to make sure, before marriage, that the chosen girl is not barren, and Njabulo had made love to her then. But the infant was very light and did not quickly grow darker as most African babies do. Already at birth there was on its head a quantity of straight, fine floss, like that which carries the seeds of certain weeds in the veld. The unfocused eyes it opened were grey flecked with yellow. Njabulo was the matt, opaque coffee-grounds colour that has always been called black; the colour of Thebedi's legs on which beaded water looked oyster-shell blue, the same colour as Thebedi's face, where the black eyes, with their interested gaze and clear whites, were so dominant.

Njabulo made no complaint. Out of his farm labourer's earnings he bought from the Indian store a cellophane-windowed pack containing a pink plastic bath, six napkins, a card of safety pins, a knitted jacket, cap and bootees, a dress, and a tin of Johnson's Baby Powder, for Thebedi's baby.

When it was two weeks old Paulus Eysendyck arrived home from the veterinary college for the holidays. He drank a glass of fresh, still-warm milk in the childhood familiarity of his mother's kitchen and heard her discussing with the old house-servant where they could get a reliable substitute to help out now that the girl Thebedi had had a baby. For the first time since he was a boy he came right into the kraal. It was eleven o'clock in the morning. The men were at work in the lands. He looked about him, urgently; the women turned away, each not wanting to be the one approached to point out where Thebedi lived. Thebedi appeared, coming slowly from the hut Njabulo had built in white-man's style, with a tin chimney, and a proper window with glass panes set in straight as walls made of unfired bricks would allow. She greeted him with hands brought together and a token movement representing the respectful bob with which she was accustomed to acknowledge she was in the presence of his father or mother. He lowered his head under the doorway of her home and went in. He said, 'I want to see. Show me.'

She had taken the bundle off her back before she came out into the light to face him. She moved between the iron bedstead made up with Njabulo's checked blankets and the small wooden table where the pink plastic bath stood among food and kitchen pots, and picked up the bundle from the snugly-blanketed grocer's box where it lay. The infant was asleep; she revealed the closed, pale, plump tiny face, with a bubble of spit at the corner of the mouth, the spidery pink hands stirring. She took off the woollen cap and the straight fine hair flew up after it in static electricity, showing gilded strands here and there. He said nothing. She was watching him as she had done when they were little, and the gang of children had trodden down a crop in their games or transgressed in some other way for which he, as the farmer's son, the white one among them, must intercede with the farmer. She disturbed the sleeping face by scratching or tickling gently at a cheek with one finger, and slowly the eyes opened, saw nothing, were still asleep, and then, awake, no longer narrowed, looked out at them, grey with yellowish flecks, his own hazel eyes.

He struggled for a moment with a grimace of tears, anger and self-pity. She could not put out her hand to him. He said, 'You haven't been near the house with it?'

She shook her head.

'Never?'

Again she shook her head.

'Don't take it out. Stay inside. Can't you take it away somewhere. You must give it to someone—'

She moved to the door with him.

He said, 'I'll see what I will do. I don't know.' And then he said: 'I feel like killing myself.'

Her eyes began to glow, to thicken with tears. For a moment there was the feeling between them that used to come when they were alone down at the river-bed.

He walked out.

Two days later, when his mother and father had left the farm for the day, he appeared again. The women were away on the lands, weeding, as they were employed to do as casual labour in summer; only the very old remained, propped up on the ground outside the huts in the flies and the sun. Thebedi did not ask him in. The child had not been well; it had diarrhoea. He asked where its food was. She said, 'The milk comes from me.' He went into Njabulo's house, where the child lay; she did not follow but stayed outside the door and watched without seeing an old crone who had lost her mind, talking to herself, talking to the fowls who ignored her.

She thought she heard small grunts from the hut, a kind of infant grunt that indicates a full stomach, a deep sleep. After a time, long or short she did not know, he came out and walked away with plodding stride (his father's gait) out of sight, towards his father's house.

The baby was not fed during the night and although she kept telling Njabulo it was sleeping, he saw for himself in the morning that it was dead. He comforted her with words and caresses. She did not cry but simply sat, staring at the door. Her hands were cold as dead chickens' feet to his touch.

Njabulo buried the little baby where farm workers were buried, in the place in the veld the farmer had given them. Some of the mounds had been left to weather away unmarked, others were covered with stones and a few had fallen wooden crosses. He was going to make a cross but before it was finished the police came and dug up the grave and took away the dead baby: someone – one of the other labourers? their women? – had reported that the baby was almost white, that, strong and healthy, it had died suddenly after a visit by the farmer's son. Pathological tests on the infant corpse showed intestinal damage not always consistent with death by natural causes.

Thebedi went for the first time to the country town where Paulus had been to school, to give evidence at the preparatory examination into the charge of murder brought against him. She cried hysterically in the witness box, saying yes, yes (the gilt hoop ear-rings swung in her ears), she saw the accused pouring liquid into the baby's mouth. She said he had threatened to shoot her if she told anyone.

More than a year went by before, in the same town, the case was brought to trial. She came to Court with a new-born baby on her back. She wore gilt hoop ear-rings; she was calm; she said she had not seen what the white man did in the house.

Paulus Eysendyck said he had visited the hut but had not poisoned the child.

The Defence did not contest that there had been a love relationship between the accused and the girl, or that intercourse had taken place, but submitted there was no proof that the child was the accused's.

The judge told the accused there was strong suspicion against him but not enough proof that he had committed the crime. The Court could not accept the girl's evidence because it was clear she had committed perjury either at this trial or at the preparatory examination. There was a suggestion in the mind of the Court that she might be an accomplice in the crime; but, again, insufficient proof.

The judge commended the honourable behaviour of the husband (sitting in court in a brown-and-yellow-quartered golf cap bought for Sundays) who had not rejected his wife and had 'even provided clothes for the unfortunate infant out of his slender means'.

The verdict on the accused was 'not guilty'.

The young white man refused to accept the congratulations of press and public and left the Court with his mother's raincoat shielding his face from photographers. His father said to the press, 'I will try and carry on as best I can to hold up my head in the district.'

Interviewed by the Sunday papers, who spelled her name in a variety of ways, the black girl, speaking in her own language, was quoted beneath her photograph: 'It was a thing of our childhood, we don't see each other any more.'

Nadine Gordimer

Glossary: *koppies* – small hill in South Africa
kraal – small village
mealie lands – maize fields
platteland – countryside
spans – an Afrikaans word meaning a team of horses or oxen
veld – open grazing land

Veronica

We had grown up together in my native village. Her family had been even poorer than mine, which was saying something in those days. Her father was a brute and her mother was weak, and since she was the eldest child a lot of the responsibility for bringing up the other children had fallen on her. From time to time I helped her out, but there was little I could do. Her father was a morbidly suspicious man. Visitors, apart from his drinking companions, were not encouraged, and I had no desire to be the cause of even more misery. I helped her fetch water from the stream and occasionally chopped firewood, but that was all. Night after night I would lie awake listening to her screams, cursing myself for my own physical inadequacy and my father for his unwillingness to become involved.

When I was twelve I started at the secondary school in the town a few miles away. During term-time I stayed with my uncle, returning to the village only during the vacations. Veronica and I remained friendly, and she was always pleased to see me, and when we could we snatched time together by the stream and she asked me endless questions about my school and the town and what I was going to be when I grew up. But for all the misery of her own life she never seemed to envy me mine.

And then came the day when I was to leave for good. I had won a scholarship to the University and I knew in my heart I would be away a long time. I was eighteen then and I thought I knew my own worth. The day before I left we met by the stream.

As she walked towards me I realised for the first time that she was no longer a girl any more but a young woman. Her clothes were still shabby and if she was no great beauty she still had a certain attractiveness that I knew would appeal to some men. Not that she was likely to meet any as long as she remained where she was. And although her father had long since stopped beating her in every other respect nothing had really altered.

'You must be happy to be going,' she said. I shrugged and pretended to be unconcerned, but of course it was the break I had hardly dared hope for.

'What about you?' I asked.

'Me!'

'Yes, why don't you get out of this place? It has nothing to offer you.'

'I can't just leave my family.'

'Why not? What have they ever done for you?'

'Don't talk like that. They are my family, that is enough.'

'But think of all the things you can do in the city,' I said.

'No, the city is for you, not me. What will I do once I get there? I have no qualifications, not even Standard Six.'

Although I knew there was a lot of truth in what she said I resisted her arguments; I suppose I was both appalled and frightened by her fatalism.

'You can go to night school and become a secretary,' I said.

She shook her head. 'I leave that to others, my own place is here.'

I snapped a twig and threw it into the water. It bobbed on the current and then vanished from sight.

'When I have qualified I will send you money to take a correspondence course,' I said. She laughed.

'Don't talk foolishness,' she said and stood up. 'I have to go and cook, my father will be home soon.'

'Here is my address. If you need anything don't hesitate to write me.' I handed her a piece of paper. She took it and tucked it in her bosom. We said goodbye and she hurried away. I thought I saw tears in her eyes as she turned to go, but I may have been mistaken.

Well, I went to the city and made good. I passed my exams and in due course I was ready to set up in a practice of my own. In all that time I did not return to the village: while I had been a student I lacked the time, and afterwards I lacked the inclination.

As soon as it was possible for me to do so I sent for my parents to come and live with me and they settled down quickly enough to their new life.

But I never forgot Veronica. She was the only person I had asked about from my mother but she had merely shrugged her shoulders and said that nothing had changed. That was the trouble with village life: nothing ever changed.

It was ten years before I made the return journey. It was in connection with my work. The government had set up a scheme whereby all the doctors in the country were obliged to put in some time in the rural districts. Quite by chance the area I was allocated included my home village, so one morning I set off with a couple of nurses, three male assistants and a suitcase full of medicines.

I was shocked by what I found. Either I had forgotten about the squalor of village life, or it had worsened during my absence. The place was crawling with disease and everybody was living – surviving, rather – in acute poverty.

I found Veronica in the same hut she had grown up in. She was squatting over a smoking fire, fanning the flames with a piece of cardboard. There was a baby tied to her back.

'Veronica,' I said. She turned round, startled. My immediate impression was that the ten years had told on her more than they should have.

'Okeke, is that you?' She peered at me through streaming eyes.

'How are you?' I asked.

'I'm still here, as you left me. What should have happened to me? Come, sit down, let me make you tea.' She indicated a stool. I watched her as she busied herself. When she finally sat down to feed the baby I asked her about herself. She shrugged.

'What am I to tell you? You heard that my parents died?'

'No, I didn't hear.'

'It's a long time now.'

'What about your brothers and sisters?'

'They are gone, all of them.'

'Where?'

'All over.' With her hand she made a semi-circle in the air.

'Do you hear from them at all?'

'What do they want with me? They have their own lives to lead.' She spoke without bitterness.

'Who is your husband?' I asked.

'You don't know him, he is not of our people.'

'How did you meet him?'

'He was in the North when the trouble broke out. They took everything he owned, he was lucky to escape alive. One day he showed up there. He had been walking for weeks and he was half-dead. I was alone here at the time. I looked after him, and when he got better he asked me to marry him. We have been together for one year now.'

'Is he good to you?'

'He is a good man. He works hard in the fields, but he has no luck.'

'I'm sorry,' I said.

'No, don't be sorry for me. We are managing, and God has blessed us with a son. Is that not enough?'

'You would be better off in the city.'

'This is my home, Okeke. But what of you? You are a big man now, not so? Where is your wife?'

'I have no wife.'

'But why?'

'All the women I meet are only interested in money and cars.'

'I don't believe you.'

'It's true.'

I was in the village a month. I saw Veronica every day, and sometimes her husband. He was a good man, as she had said, if a bit simple. On the day I left I had to force her to accept a present of some money. It was as much as I could afford, but not as much as I would have liked to have been able to give her.

A few months after I got back to the city the war broke out. As she was in the fighting zone I lost contact with her again.

Three years passed before I could travel to the village. This time I went alone. When I got there and saw all the destruction I could have wept. I had never imagined anything like it. I went straight to Veronica's hut. It was dark inside and bare save for a figure huddled on a mat on the ground.

'Veronica,' I called. She opened her eyes. I went over and knelt beside her. My eyes had become accustomed to the darkness. I saw at once that if I did not get her out of there quickly she would die.

'Okeke, welcome,' she said. I reached for her hand and held it. It was cold and limp.

'I'll get you out of here, don't worry,' I said.

'What for?'

'Veronica, if you stay here you'll die.'

She tried to sit up but I restrained her. 'Don't exert yourself, you need all your strength.'

'I was lying here thinking about you. I wanted to see you once more before I go.'

'I'm here now, and you're going to be all right.'

'Okeke, I won't live to see tomorrow. Nor do I want to. My husband is dead, and my child also. There is nothing left for me in this world.'

'You're still a young woman, in time you will forget this.'

'No, Okeke, listen to me. I don't want to live, you hear? Now that I have seen you I am happy. Go, and leave me in peace.'

She closed her eyes and turned her face to the wall. I gathered her up in my arms. She weighed no more than a ten-year-old child. She was dead before I reached my car.

I cried that night for the terrible waste. In the morning, just as the sun was rising, I carried her body down to the stream. And then I dug her a grave and buried her and afterwards I watched the flow of the stream until it was time for me to go away for the last time.

Adewale Maja-Pearce

The Schoolteacher's Guest

The Schoolteacher Ines entered The Pearl of the Orient, deserted at this hour, walked to the counter where Riad Halabi was rolling up a bolt of bright-flowered cloth, and announced to him that she had just cut off the head of a guest in her boarding house. The merchant took out his white handkerchief and clapped it to his mouth.

'What did you say, Ines?'

'Exactly what you heard, Turk.'

'Is he dead?'

'Of course.'

'And now what are you going to do?'

'That's what I came to ask you,' she replied, tucking back a stray lock of hair.

'I think I'd better close the store,' sighed Riad Halabi.

The two had known each other so long that neither could remember the exact number of years, although both recalled every detail of the day their friendship had begun. At the time, Halabi had been one of those salesmen who wander the byways offering their wares, a commercial pilgrim without compass or fixed course, an Arab immigrant with a false Turkish passport, lonely, weary, with a palate split like a rabbit's and a subsequent longing to sit in the shadows. She had been a still-young woman with firm hips and proud shoulders, the town's only schoolteacher, and the mother of a twelve-year-old son born of a fleeting love affair. The boy was the centre of the schoolteacher's life; she cared for him with unwavering devotion but, barely masking her inclination to indulge him, applied to him the same norms of discipline she demanded of the other schoolchildren. She did not want anyone to be able to say she had brought him up badly; at the same time, she hoped to negate the father's legacy of waywardness and instead form her son to be of clear mind and generous heart. The very evening on which Riad Halabi had driven into Agua Santa from one side of town, from the other a group of boys had carried in the body of schoolteacher Ines's son on an improvised stretcher. He had walked on to someone's property to pick up a fallen mango, and the owner, an outsider whom no one really knew, had fired a blast from his rifle meaning to scare the boy away but drilling a black hole in the middle of his forehead through which his life rapidly escaped. At that moment, the salesman had discovered his vocation for leadership and, without knowing how, had found himself at the centre of things, consoling the mother, organizing the funeral as if he were a member of the family, and calming the people to prevent them from tearing the perpetrator limb from limb. Meanwhile, the murderer, realizing that his life would be worth very little if he remained here, had fled, never meaning to return.

It was Riad Halabi who, the following morning, was at the head of the crowd that marched from the cemetery to the place where the boy had fallen. All the inhabitants of Agua Santa had spent that day hauling mangoes, which they threw through the windows until the house was filled from floor to ceiling. After a few weeks, the sun had fermented the fruit, which burst open spilling a viscous juice and impregnating the walls with a golden blood, a sweetish pus, that transformed the dwelling into a fossil of prehistoric dimensions, an enormous beast in process of putrefaction, tormented by the infinite diligence of the larvae and mosquitoes of decomposition.

The death of the boy, the role he had played during those days, and the welcome he had received in Agua Santa, had determined the course of Riad Halabi's life. He forgot his nomadic ancestry and remained in the village. There he opened a business, The Pearl of the Orient. He married, was widowed, married a second time, and continued his trade, while his reputation for being a just man steadily increased. Ines, in turn, educated several generations of children with the tenacious affection she would have bestowed upon her son, until her energies were spent; then she had stepped aside for the teachers who arrived from the city with new primers, and retired. After leaving the schoolroom, she felt as if she had aged suddenly, as if time were accelerating; the days passed so quickly that she could not remember where the hours had gone.

'I go around in a daze, Turk. I'm dying and don't even know it,' she commented.

'You're as healthy as you ever were, Ines,' replied Riad Halabi. 'The problem is that you're bored. You should not be idle.' And he suggested that she add a few rooms to her house and take in guests: 'We don't have a hotel in this town.'

'We don't have tourists, either,' she added.

'A clean bed and warm breakfast are a blessing for travellers.'

And so they had been, primarily for the truckdrivers for National Petroleum, who stayed the night in her boarding house when the fatigue and tedium of the road had filled their heads with hallucinations.

The schoolteacher Ines was the most respected matron in all Agua Santa. She had taught the town's children for several decades, which granted her the authority to intervene in all their lives and take them by the ear when she felt it necessary. Girls brought their boyfriends for her approval, husbands and wives came to her with their marital disagreements; she was counsellor, arbiter, and judge in all the town's problems. Her authority, in fact, was mightier than that of the priest, the doctor, or the police. No one stopped her from the exercise of that power. On one occasion she had stalked into the jail, passed the Lieutenant without speaking, snatched the keys from a nail on the wall, and removed from a cell one of her students who had been jailed after a drunken spree. The officer tried to stand in her way, but she shoved him aside and marched the boy outside by the back of his collar. Once in the street, she had given him a couple of smacks and assured him that the next time this happened she would lower his pants and give him a spanking he would never forget. The day that Ines came to tell Riad Halabi she had killed one of her clients, he did not doubt for a moment that she was serious, because he knew her too well. He took her arm and walked with her the two blocks that separated The Pearl of the Orient from her house. It was one of the grandest buildings in town, adobe and wood, with a wide veranda where hammocks were hung during the hottest siestas, and ceiling fans in every room. At that hour the house seemed to be empty; only one guest sat in the parlour drinking beer, mesmerized by the television.

'Where is he?' whispered the Arab merchant.

'In one of the back rooms,' Ines replied, not even lowering her voice.

She led him to the row of rooms she rented – all joined by an arcade with purple morning glories climbing the columns and pots of ferns hanging from the beams – bordering a patio planted with medlar and banana trees. Ines opened the last door and Riad Halabi entered a room in deep shadow. The shutters were closed, and it was a moment before he saw on the bed the corpse of an inoffensive-looking old man, a decrepit stranger swimming in the puddle of his own death, his trousers stained with excrement, his head hanging by a strip of ashen flesh, and wearing a terrible expression of distress, as if apologizing for all the disturbance and blood, and for the uncommon bother of having allowed himself to be murdered. Riad Halabi sat down on the room's only chair, his eyes on the floor, trying to control the lurch of his stomach. Ines remained standing, arms across her chest, calculating that it would take her two days to wash out the stains and at least two more to rid the room of its odour of faeces and fear.

'How did you do it?' Riad Halabi asked finally, wiping the sweat from his forehead.

'With the machete for harvesting coconuts. I came up behind him and lopped off his head with one swing. He never knew what hit him, poor man.'

'Why?'

'I had to do it. It was fate. This old man had very bad luck. He never meant to stop in Agua Santa; he was driving through the town and a rock shattered his windshield. He came to pass a few hours here while the Italian down at the garage found another windshield. He's changed a lot – we've all grown older, I guess but I recognized him instantly. I've been waiting all these years; I knew he would come sooner or later. He's the man with the mangoes.'

'May Allah protect us,' murmured Riad Halabi.

'Do you think we should call the Lieutenant?'

'Not on your life; why do you say that?'

'I'm in the right, he killed my boy.'

'The Lieutenant wouldn't understand that, Ines.'

'An eye for an eye and a tooth for a tooth, Turk. Isn't that what your religion teaches?'

'But that's not how the law works, Ines.'

'Well, then, we can fix him up a little and say he committed suicide.'

'Don't touch him. How many guests do you have in the house?'

'Just that truckdriver. He'll be on his way as soon as it's cool; he had to drive to the capital.'

'Good. Don't take in any more guests. Lock the door to this room and wait for me. I'll be back tonight.'

'What are you doing to do?'

'I'll take care of this in my own way.'

Riad Halabi was sixty-five years old, but he had conserved his youthful vigour and the same spirit that had positioned him at the head of the throng the day he arrived in Agua Santa. He left the schoolteacher's house and walked rapidly to the first of several visits he was to make that afternoon. Soon after, a persistent murmur began to spread through the town. The inhabitants of Agua Santa wakened from the lethargy of years, excited by the unbelievable news that was being repeated from house to house, an insuppressible buzzing, information that strained to be uttered in shouts, gossip that by the very need to be held to a murmur was conferred special status. Before sunset you could sense in the air the restless elation that for several years would be a characteristic of the town, one incomprehensible to strangers passing through, who could find nothing extraordinary in this town which had the appearance of being an insignificant backwater like so many others on the edge of the jungle. Early in the evening, men started arriving at the tavern; women carried their kitchen chairs out to the sidewalk and sat down to enjoy the cool air; young people gathered en masse in the plaza, as if it were Sunday. The Lieutenant and his men casually made their rounds and then accepted the invitation of the girls at the whorehouse who were celebrating a birthday, they said. By nightfall there were more people in the street than on All Saints' Day; all of them were so studiously occupied in their activities that they seemed to be practising a part in a movie: some were playing dominoes, others were drinking rum and smoking on the street corners, some couples were out for a stroll, hand in hand, mothers were running after their children, grandmothers peering nosily from open doorways. The priest lighted the lamps in the parish church and rang the bells signalling a novena to Saint Isidro Martyr, but no one was in the mood for that kind of devotion.

At nine-thirty there was a meeting in the house of schoolteacher Ines: the Turk, the town doctor, and four young men she had taught from the first grade and who were now hefty veterans back from military service. Riad Halabi led them to the back room, where they found the cadaver covered with insects: the window had been left open and it was the hour of the mosquitoes. They stuffed the victim in a canvas sack, wrestled it out to the street, and unceremoniously threw it into the back of Riad Halabi's truck. They drove through the town, right down the main street, waving, as usual, to anyone they happened to see. Some neighbours returned their salutation with more than ordinary enthusiasm, while others pretended not to notice them, furtively giggling, like children surprised at some mischief. Beneath brilliant moonlight the men drove to the spot where many years before the son of the schoolteacher Ines had stooped down for the last time to pick up a mango. The overgrown property sat amid the malign weeds of neglect, decayed by time and bad memories, a tangled hill where mangoes had grown wild, where fruit had dropped from the trees and taken root in the ground, giving birth to new clumps that had in turn engendered others, until an impenetrable jungle had been created that had swallowed up fences, path, even the ruins of the house, of which only a lingering trace of the odour of marmalade remained. The men lighted their kerosene lanterns and plunged into the dense growth, hacking a path with their machetes. When they felt they had gone far enough, one of them pointed to a spot and there, at the foot of a gigantic tree weighed down with fruit, they dug a deep hole in which they deposited the canvas sack. Before shovelling back the dirt, Riad Halabi spoke a brief Muslim prayer, because he knew no other. When they got back to town at midnight, they found that no one had gone to bed; lights were blazing in every window, and people were circulating through the streets.

Meanwhile, the schoolteacher Ines had scrubbed the walls, and furniture in the back room with soap and water; she had burned the bedclothing, aired the house, and was waiting for her friends with a fine dinner and a pitcher of rum and pineapple juice. The meal was eaten to the accompaniment of merry chatter about the latest cockfights – a barbaric sport according to the schoolteacher, but less barbaric, the men alleged, than the bullfights in which a Colombian matador had just lost his liver. Riad Halabi was the last to say goodbye. That night, for the first time in his life, he felt odd. At the door, the schoolteacher Ines took his hands and for a moment held them in hers.

'Thank you, Turk,' she said.

'Why did you come to me, Ines?'

'Because you are the person I love most in this world, and because you should have been the father of my son.'

The next day the inhabitants of Agua Santa returned to their usual chores exalted by a magnificent complicity, by a secret kept by good neighbours, one they would guard with absolute zeal and pass down for many years as a legend of justice, until the death of the schoolteacher Ines freed us, and now I can tell the story.

Isabel Allende

The Gold Cadillac

My sister and I were playing out on the front lawn when the gold Cadillac rolled up and my father stepped from behind the wheel. We ran to him, our eyes filled with wonder. 'Daddy, whose Cadillac?' I asked.

And Wilma demanded, 'Where's our Mercury?'

My father grinned. 'Go get your mother and I'll tell you all about it.'

'Is it ours?' I cried. 'Daddy, is it ours?'

'Get your mother!' he laughed. 'And tell her to hurry!'

Wilma and I ran off to obey as Mr Pondexter next door came from his house to see what this new Cadillac was all about. We threw open the front door, ran through the downstairs front parlour and straight through the house to the kitchen where my mother was cooking and one of my aunts was helping her. 'Come on, Mother-Dear!' we cried together. 'Daddy say come on out and see this new car!'

'What?' said my mother, her face showing her surprise. 'What're you talking about?'

'A Cadillac!' I cried.

'He said hurry up!' relayed Wilma.

And then we took off again, up the back stairs to the second floor of the duplex. Running down the hall, we banged on all the apartment doors. My uncles and their wives stepped to the doors. It was good it was a Saturday morning. Everybody was home.

'We got us a Cadillac! We got us a Cadillac!' Wilma and I proclaimed in unison. We had decided that the Cadillac had to be ours if our father was driving it and holding on to the keys. 'Come on see!' Then we raced on, through the upstairs sunroom, down the front steps, through the downstairs sunroom, and out to the Cadillac. Mr Pondexter was still there. Mr LeRoy and Mr Courtland from down the street were there too and all were admiring the Cadillac as my father stood proudly by, pointing out the various features.

'Brand-new 1950 Coup deVille!' I heard one of the men saying.

'Just off the showroom floor!' my father said. 'I just couldn't resist it.'

My sister and I eased up to the car and peeked in. It was all gold inside. Gold leather seats. Gold carpeting. Gold dashboard. It was like no car we had owned before. It looked like a car for rich folks.

'Daddy, are we rich?' I asked. My father laughed.

'Daddy, it's ours, isn't it?' asked Wilma, who was older and more practical than I. She didn't intend to give her heart too quickly to something that wasn't hers.

'You like it?'

'Oh, Daddy, yes!'

He looked at me. 'What 'bout you, 'lois?'

'Yes, sir!'

My father laughed again. 'Then I expect I can't much disappoint my girls, can I? It's ours all right!'

Wilma and I hugged our father with our joy. My uncles came from the house and my aunts, carrying their babies, came out too. Everybody surrounded the car and owwed and ahhed. Nobody could believe it.

Then my mother came out.

Everybody stood back grinning as she approached the car. There was no smile on her face. We all waited for her to speak. She stared at the car, then looked at my father, standing there as proud as he could be. Finally she said, 'You didn't buy this car, did you, Wilbert?'

'Gotta admit I did. Couldn't resist it.'

'But . . . but what about our Mercury? It was perfectly good!'

'Don't you like the Cadillac, Dee?'

'That Mercury wasn't even a year old!'

My father nodded. 'And I'm sure whoever buys it is going to get themselves a good car. But we've got ourselves a better one. Now stop frowning, honey, and let's take ourselves a ride in our brand-new Cadillac!'

My mother shook her head. 'I've got food on the stove,' she said and turning away walked back to the house.

There was an awkward silence and then my father said, 'You know Dee never did much like surprises. Guess this here Cadillac was a bit too much for her. I best go smooth things out with her.'

Everybody watched as he went after my mother. But when he came back, he was alone.

'Well, what she say?' asked one of my uncles.

My father shrugged and smiled. 'Told me I bought this Cadillac alone, I could just ride in it alone.'

Another uncle laughed. 'Uh-oh! Guess she told you!'

'Oh, she'll come around,' said one of my aunts. 'Any woman would be proud to ride in this car.'

'That's what I'm banking on,' said my father as he went around to the street side of the car and opened the door. 'All right! Who's for a ride?'

'We are!' Wilma and I cried.

All three of my uncles and one of my aunts, still holding her baby, and Mr Pondexter climbed in with us and we took off for the first ride in the gold Cadillac. It was a glorious ride and we drove all through the city of Toledo. We rode past the church and past the school. We rode through Ottawa Hills where the rich folks lived and on into Walbridge Park and past the zoo, then along the Maumee River. But none of us had had enough of the car so my father put the car on the road and we drove all the way to Detroit. We had plenty of family there and everybody was just as pleased as could be about the Cadillac. My father told our Detroit relatives that he was in the doghouse with my mother about buying the Cadillac. My uncles told them she wouldn't ride in the car. All the Detroit family thought that was funny and everybody, including my father, laughed about it and said my mother would come around.

It was early evening by the time we got back home, and I could see from my mother's face she had not come around. She was angry now not only about the car, but that we had been gone so long. I didn't understand that, since my father had called her as soon as we reached Detroit to let her know where we were. I had heard him myself. I didn't understand either why she did not like that fine Cadillac and thought she was being terribly disagreeable with my father. That night as she tucked Wilma and me in bed I told her that too.

'Is this your business?' she asked.

'Well, I just think you ought to be nice to Daddy. I think you ought to ride in that car with him! It'd sure make him happy.'

'I think you ought to go to sleep,' she said and turned out the light.

Later I heard her arguing with my father. 'We're supposed to be saving for a house!' she said.

'We've already got a house!' said my father.

'But you said you wanted a house in a better neighbourhood. I thought that's what we both said!'

'I haven't changed my mind.'

'Well, you have a might funny way of saving for it, then. Your brothers are saving for houses of their own and you don't see them out buying new cars every year!'

'We'll still get the house, Dee. That's a promise!'

'Not with new Cadillacs we won't!' said my mother and then she said a very loud good night and all was quiet.

The next day was Sunday and everybody figured that my mother would be sure to give in and ride in the Cadillac. After all, the family always went to church together on

Sunday. But she didn't give in. What was worse she wouldn't let Wilma and me ride in the Cadillac either. She took us each by the hand, walked past the Cadillac where my father stood waiting and headed on towards the church, three blocks away. I was really mad at her now. I had been looking forward to driving up to the church in that gold Cadillac and having everybody see.

On most Sunday afternoons during the summertime, my mother, my father, Wilma, and I would go for a ride. Sometimes we just rode around the city and visited friends and family. Sometimes we made short trips over to Chicago or Peoria or Detroit to see relatives there or to Cleveland where we had relatives too, but we could also see the Cleveland Indians play. Sometimes we joined our aunts and uncles and drove in a caravan out to the park or to the beach. At the park or the beach Wilma and I would run and play. My mother and my aunts would spread a picnic and my father and my uncles would shine their cars.

But on this Sunday afternoon my mother refused to ride anywhere. She told Wilma and me that we could go. So we left her alone in the big, empty house, and the family cars, led by the gold Cadillac, headed for the park. For a while I played and had a good time, but then I stopped playing and went to sit with my father. Despite his laughter he seemed sad to me. I think he was missing my mother as much as I was.

That evening my father took my mother to dinner down at the corner café. They walked. Wilma and I stayed at the house chasing fireflies in the back yard. My aunts and uncles sat in the yard and on the porch talking and laughing about the day and watching us. It was a soft summer's evening, the kind that came every day and was expected. The smell of charcoal and of barbecue drifting from up the block, the sound of laughter and music and talk drifting from yard to yard were all a part of it. Soon one of my uncles joined Wilma and me in our chase of fireflies and when my mother and father came home we were at it still. My mother and father watched us for a while, while everybody else watched them to see if my father would take out the Cadillac and if my mother would slide in beside him to take a ride. But it soon became evident that the dinner had not changed my mother's mind. She still refused to ride in the Cadillac. I just couldn't understand her objection to it.

Though my mother didn't like the Cadillac, everybody else in the neighbourhood certainly did. That meant quite a few folks too, since we lived in a very busy block. On one corner was a grocery store, a cleaner's and a gas station. Across the street was a beauty shop and a fish market, and down the street was a bar, another grocery store, the Dixie Theatre, the café, and a drugstore. There were always people strolling to or from one of these places and because our house was right in the middle of the block just about everybody had to pass our house and the gold Cadillac. Sometimes people took in the Cadillac as they walked, their heads turning for a longer look as they passed. Then there were people who just outright stopped and took a good look before continuing on their way. I was proud to say that car belonged to my family. I felt mighty important as people called to me as I ran down the street. ''Ey, 'lois! How's that Cadillac, girl? Riding fine?' I told my mother how much everybody liked that car. She was not impressed and made no comment.

Since just about everybody on the block knew everybody else, most folks knew that my mother wouldn't ride in the Cadillac. Because of that, my father took a lot of good-natured kidding from the men. My mother got kidded too as the women said if she didn't ride in that car, maybe some other woman would. And everybody laughed about it and began to bet on who would give in first, my mother or my father. But then my father said he was going to drive the car south into Mississippi to visit my grandparents and everybody stopped laughing.

My uncles stopped.

So did my aunts.

Everybody.

'Look here, Wilbert,' said one of my uncles, 'it's too dangerous. It's like putting a loaded gun to your head.'

'I paid good money for that car,' said my father. 'That gives me a right to drive it where I please. Even down to Mississippi.'

My uncles argued with him and tried to talk him out of driving the car south. So did my aunts and so did the neighbours, Mr LeRoy, Mr Courtland and Mr Pondexter. They said it was a dangerous thing, a mighty dangerous thing, for a black man to drive an expensive car into the rural South.

'Not much those folks hate more'n to see a northern Negro coming down there in a fine car,' said Mr Pondexter. 'They see those Ohio licence plates, they'll figure you coming down uppity, trying to lord your fine car over them!'

I listened, but I didn't understand. I didn't understand why they didn't want my father to drive that car south. It was his.

'Listen to Pondexter, Wilbert!' cried another uncle. 'We might've fought a war to free people overseas, but we're not free here! Man, those white folks down south'll lynch you soon's look at you. You know that!'

Wilma and I looked at each other. Neither of us knew what *lynch* meant, but the word sent a shiver through us. We held each other's hand.

My father was silent, then he said: 'All my life I've had to be heedful of what white folks thought. Well, I'm tired of that. I worked hard for everything I got. Got it honest, too. Now I got that Cadillac because I liked it and because it meant something to me that somebody like me from Mississippi could go and buy it. It's my car, I paid for it, and I'm driving it south.'

My mother, who had said nothing through all this, now stood. 'Then the girls and I'll be going too,' she said.

'No!' said my father.

My mother only looked at him and went off to the kitchen.

My father shook his head. It seemed he didn't want us to go. My uncles looked at each other, then at my father. 'You set on doing this, we'll all go,' they said. 'That way we can watch out for each other.' My father took a moment and nodded. Then my aunts got up and went off to their kitchens too.

All the next day my aunts and my mother cooked and the house was filled with delicious smells. They fried chicken and baked hams and cakes and sweet potato pies and mixed potato salad. They filled jugs with water and punch and coffee. Then they packed everything in huge picnic baskets along with bread and boiled eggs, oranges and apples, plates and napkins, spoons and forks and cups. They placed all that food on the back seats of the cars. It was like a grand, grand picnic we were going on, and Wilma and I were mighty excited. We could hardly wait to start.

My father, my mother, Wilma and I got into the Cadillac. My uncles, my aunts, my cousins got into the Ford, the Buick, and the Chevrolet, and we rolled off in our caravan headed south. Though my mother was finally riding in the Cadillac, she had no praise for it. In fact, she said nothing about it at all. She still seemed upset and since she still seemed to feel the same about the car, I wondered why she had insisted upon making this trip with my father.

We left the city of Toledo behind, drove through Bowling Green and down through the Ohio countryside of farms and small towns, through Dayton and Cincinnati, and across the Ohio River into Kentucky. On the other side of the river my father stopped the car and looked back at Wilma and me and said, 'Now from here on, whenever we stop and there're white people around, I don't want either one of you to say a word. *Not one word!* Your mother and I'll do all the talking. That understood?'

'Yes, sir,' Wilma and I both said, though we didn't truly understand why.

My father nodded, looked at my mother and started the car again. We rolled on, down Highway 25 and through the bluegrass hills of Kentucky. Soon we began to see signs. Signs that read: WHITE ONLY, COLOURED NOT ALLOWED. Hours later, we left the Bluegrass State and crossed into Tennessee. Now we saw even more of the signs saying: WHITE ONLY, COLOURED NOT ALLOWED. We saw the signs above water fountains and in restaurant windows. We saw them in ice-cream parlours and at hamburger stands. We saw them in front of hotels and motels, and on the restroom door of filling stations. I didn't like the signs. I felt as if I were in a foreign land.

I couldn't understand why the signs were there and I asked my father what the signs meant. He said they meant we couldn't drink from the water fountains. He said they meant we couldn't stop to sleep in the motels. He said they meant we couldn't stop to eat in the restaurants. I looked at the grand picnic basket I had been enjoying so much. Now I understood why my mother had packed it. Suddenly the picnic did not seem so grand.

Finally we reached Memphis. We got there at a bad time. Traffic was heavy and we got separated from the rest of the family. We tried to find them but it was no use. We had to go on alone. We reached the Mississippi state line and soon after we heard a police siren. A police car came up behind us. My father slowed the Cadillac, then stopped. Two white policemen got out of their car. They eyeballed the Cadillac and told my father to get out.

'Whose car is this, boy?' they asked.

I saw anger in my father's eyes. 'It's mine,' he said.

'You're a liar,' said one of the policemen. 'You stole this car.'

'Turn around, put your hands on top of that car and spread-eagle,' said the other policeman.

My father did as he was told. They searched him and I didn't understand why. I didn't understand either why they had called my father a liar and didn't believe that the Cadillac was his. I wanted to ask but I remembered my father's warning not to say a word and I obeyed that warning.

The policemen told my father to get in the back of the police car. My father did. One policeman got back in the police car. The other policeman slid behind the wheel of our Cadillac. The police car started off. The Cadillac followed. Wilma and I looked at each other and at our mother. We didn't know what to think. We were scared.

The Cadillac followed the police car into a small town and stopped in front of the police station. The policeman stepped out of our Cadillac and took the keys. The other policeman took my father into the police station.

'Mother-Dear!' Wilma and I cried. 'What're they going to do to our daddy? They going to hurt him?'

'He'll be all right,' said my mother. 'He'll be all right.' But she didn't sound so sure of that. She seemed worried.

We waited. More than three hours we waited. Finally my father came out of the police station. We had lots of questions to ask him. He said the police had given him a ticket for speeding and locked him up. But then the judge had come. My father had paid the ticket and they had let him go.

He started the Cadillac and drove slowly out of the town, below the speed limit. The police car followed us. People standing on steps and sitting on porches and in front of stores stared at us as we passed. Finally we were out of the town. The police car still followed. Dusk was falling. The night grew black and finally the police car turned around and left us.

We drove and drove. But my father was tired now and my grandparents' farm was still far away. My father said he had to get some sleep and since my mother didn't drive, he pulled into a grove of trees at the side of the road and stopped.

'I'll keep watch,' said my mother.

'Wake me if you see anybody,' said my father.

'Just rest,' said my mother.

So my father slept. But that bothered me. I needed him awake. I was afraid of the dark and of the woods and of whatever lurked there. My father was the one who kept us safe, he and my uncles. But already the police had taken my father away from us once today and my uncles were lost.

'Go to sleep, baby,' said my mother. 'Go to sleep.'

But I was afraid to sleep until my father woke. I had to help my mother keep watch. I figured I had to help protect us too, in case the police came back and tried to take my father away again. There was a long, sharp knife in the picnic basket and I took hold of it, clutching it tightly in my hand. Ready to strike, I sat there in the back of the car, eyes wide, searching the blackness outside the Cadillac. Wilma, for a while, searched the night too, then she fell asleep. I didn't want to sleep, but soon I found I couldn't help myself as an unwelcome drowsiness came over me. I had an uneasy sleep and when I woke it was dawn and my father was gently shaking me. I woke with a start and my hand went up, but the knife wasn't there. My mother had it.

My father took my hand. 'Why were you holding the knife, 'lois?' he asked.

I looked at him and at my mother. 'I—I was scared,' I said.

My father was thoughtful. 'No need to be scared now sugar,' he said. 'Daddy's here and so is Mother-Dear.' Then after a glance at my mother, he got out of the car, walked to the road, looked down it one way, then the other. When he came back and started the motor, he turned the Cadillac north, not south.

'What're you doing?' asked my mother.

'Heading back to Memphis,' said my father. 'Cousin Halton's there. We'll leave the Cadillac and get his car. Driving this car any farther south with you and the girls in the car, it's just not worth the risk.'

And so that's what we did. Instead of driving through Mississippi in golden splendour, we travelled its streets and roads and highways in Cousin Halton's solid, yet not so splendid, four-year-old Chevy. When we reached my grandparents' farm, my uncles and aunts were already there. Everybody was glad to see us. They had been worried. They asked about the Cadillac. My father told them what had happened, and they nodded and said he had done the best thing.

We stayed one week in Mississippi. During that week I often saw my father, looking deep in thought, walking off alone across the family land. I saw my mother watching him. One day I ran after my father, took his hand, and walked the land with him. I asked him all the questions that were on my mind. I asked him why the policemen had treated him the way they had and why people didn't want us to eat in the restaurants or drink from the water fountains or sleep in the hotels. I told him I just didn't understand all that.

My father looked at me and said that it all was a difficult thing to understand and he didn't really understand it himself. He said it all had to do with the fact that black people had once been forced to be slaves. He said it had to do with our skins being coloured. He said it had to do with stupidity and ignorance. He said it had to do with the law, the law that said we could be treated like this here in the South. And for that matter, he added, any other place in these United States where folks thought the same as so many folks did here in the South. But he also said, 'I'm hoping one day though we can drive that long road down here and there won't be any signs. I'm hoping one day the police won't stop us just because of the colour of our skins and we're riding in a gold Cadillac with northern plates.'

When the week ended, we said a sad good-bye to my grandparents and all the Mississippi family and headed in a caravan back to Memphis. In Memphis we returned Cousin Halton's car and got our Cadillac. Once we were home my father put the Cadillac in the garage and didn't drive it. I didn't hear my mother say any more about the Cadillac. I didn't hear my father speak of it either.

Some days passed and then on a bright Saturday afternoon while Wilma and I were playing in the back yard, I saw my father go into the garage. He opened the garage doors wide so the sunshine streamed in, and began to shine the Cadillac. I saw my mother at the kitchen window staring out across the yard at my father. For a long time, she stood there watching my father shine his car. Then she came out and crossed the yard to the garage and I heard her say, 'Wilbert, you keep the car.'

He looked at her as if he had not heard.

'You keep it,' she repeated and turned and walked back to the house.

My father watched her until the back door had shut behind her. Then he went on shining the car and soon began to sing. About an hour later he got into the car and drove away. That evening when he came back he was walking. The Cadillac was nowhere in sight.

'Daddy, where's our new Cadillac?' I demanded to know. So did Wilma.

He smiled and put his hand on my head. 'Sold it,' he said as my mother came into the room.

'But how come?' I asked. 'We poor now?'

'No, sugar. We've got more money towards our new house now and we're all together. I figure that makes us about the richest folks in the world.' He smiled at my mother and she smiled too and came into his arms.

After that we drove around in an old 1930s Model Ford my father had. He said he'd factory-ordered us another Mercury, this time with my mother's approval. Despite that, most folks on the block figured we had fallen on hard times after such a splashy showing of good times and some folks even laughed at us as the Ford rattled around the city. I must admit that at first I was pretty much embarrassed to be riding around in that old Ford after the splendour of the Cadillac. But my father said to hold my head high. We and the family knew the truth. As fine as the Cadillac had been, he said, it had pulled us apart for a while. Now, as ragged and noisy as that old Ford was, we all rode in it together and we were a family again. So I held my head high.

Still though, I often thought of that Cadillac. We had had the Cadillac only a little more than a month, but I wouldn't soon forget its splendour or how I'd felt riding around inside it. I wouldn't soon forget either the ride we had taken south in it. I wouldn't soon forget the signs, the policemen, or my fear. I would remember that ride and the gold Cadillac all my life.

Mildred Taylor

A Stench of Kerosene

Outside, a mare neighed. Guleri recognised the neighing and ran out of the house. The mare was from her parents' village. She put her head against its neck as if it were the door to her father's house.

Guleri's parents lived in Chamba. A few miles from her husband's village which was on high ground, the road curved and descended steeply downhill. From this point one could see Chamba lying a long way away at one's feet. Whenever Guleri was homesick she would take her husband, Manak, and go up to this point. She would see the homes of Chamba twinkling in the sunlight and would come back, her heart glowing with pride.

Once every year, after the harvest had been gathered in, Guleri was allowed to spend a few days with her parents. They sent a man to Lakarmandi to bring her back to Chamba. Two of her friends, who were also married to boys who lived away from Chamba, came home at the same time and the girls looked forward to their annual reunion, talking about their joys and sorrow. They went about the streets together. Then there was the harvest festival when the girls would have new clothes made for the occasion. Their *dupattas* would be dyed, starched and sprinkled with mica to make them glisten. They would buy glass bangles and silver ear-rings.

Guleri always counted the days to the harvest. When autumn breezes cleared the skies of monsoon clouds she thought of little else. She went about her daily chores – fed the cattle, cooked food for her parents-in-law – and then sat back to work out how long it would be before someone came to fetch her from her parents' village.

And now, once again, it was time for her annual visit. She caressed the mare joyfully, greeted her father's servant, Natu, and made preparations to leave the next day. She did not have to express her excitement in words; the look on her face was enough. Her husband pulled at his *hookah* and closed his eyes. It seemed as if he either did not like the tobacco or that he could not bear to face his wife.

'You'll come to the fair at Chamba, won't you? Come even for a day,' she pleaded.

Manak put aside his *chillum* but did not reply. 'Why don't you answer me?' she asked, a little cross. 'Shall I tell you something?'

'I know what you're going to say – that you only go to your parents once a year. Well you've never been stopped before.'

'Then why do you want to stop me this time?' she demanded.

'Just this once,' he pleaded.

'Your mother's said nothing so why do you stand in the way?' Guleri was childishly stubborn.

'My mother . . .' Manak did not finish his sentence.

On the long-awaited morning, Guleri was ready long before dawn. She had no children and therefore no problem of having to leave them behind or take them with her. Natu saddled the mare as she took leave of Manak's parents. They patted her head and blessed her.

'I'll come with you for part of the way,' Manak said.

Guleri was happy as they set out. She hid Manak's flute under her dupatta.

After the village of Khajiar, the road descended steeply to Chamba. There she took out the flute and gave it to him. She took his hand in hers and said, 'Come now, play your flute.' But Manak, lost in his thoughts, paid no heed. 'Why don't you play your flute?' she asked, coaxing him. He looked at her sadly. Then putting the flute to his lips, blew a strange anguished wail.

'Guleri, don't go away,' he begged her. 'I ask again, don't go away this time.' He handed the flute to her, unable to continue.

'But why?' she asked. 'Come over on the day of the fair and we'll return together, I promise you.'

Manak did not ask again.

They stopped by the roadside. Natu took the mare a few paces ahead to leave the couple alone. It crossed Manak's mind that it was at this time of the year, seven years ago, that he and his friends had come on this very road to go to the harvest festival in Chamba. And it was at this fair that Manak had first seen Guleri and they had bartered their hearts to each other. Later, managing to meet her alone, he remembered taking her hand and telling her, 'You are like unripe corn – full of milk.'

'Cattle go for unripe corn,' Guleri had replied, freeing her hand with a jerk. 'Human beings prefer it roasted. If you want me, go and ask my father for my hand.'

Among Manak's kinsmen it was customary to settle the bride price before the wedding. Manak was nervous because he did not know the price Guleri's father would demand from him. But Guleri's father was prosperous and had lived in cities. He had sworn that he could not take money for his daughter but would give her to a worthy young man from a good family. Manak, he decided, answered these requirements and soon after, Guleri and Manak were married. Deep in memories, Manak was roused by Guleri's hand on his shoulder.

'What are you dreaming of?' she teased him.

He did not answer. The mare neighed impatiently and Guleri got up to leave. 'Do you know the bluebell wood a couple of miles from here?' she asked. 'It's said that anyone who goes through it becomes deaf. You must have passed through that bluebell wood. You don't seem to be hearing anything I say.'

'You're right, Guleri. I can't hear anything you're saying to me,' and Manak sighed.

They looked at each other. Neither understood the other's thoughts. 'I'll go now,' Guleri said gently. 'You'd better go back. You've come a long way from home.'

'You've walked all the distance. You'd better get on the mare,' replied Manak.

'Here, take your flute.'

'You take it.'

'Will you come and play it on the day of the fair?' she asked with a smile. The sun shone in her eyes. Manak turned his face away. Perplexed, Guleri shrugged her shoulders and took the road to Chamba. Manak returned home.

He entered the house and slumped listlessly on the *charpoy*. 'You've been away a long time,' exclaimed his mother. 'Did you go all the way to Chamba?'

'Not all the way, only to the top of the hill.' Manak's voice was heavy.

'Why do you croak like an old woman?' said his mother severely. 'Be a man.'

Manak wanted to retort, 'You are a woman; why don't you cry like one for a change!' But he remained silent.

Manak and Guleri had been married seven years but she had never borne a child and Manak's mother had made a secret resolve that she would not let it go beyond the eighth year. This year, true to her decision, she had paid five hundred rupees to get him a second wife and she was waiting, as Manak knew, for Guleri to go to her parents before bringing in the new bride. Obedient to his mother and to custom, Manak's body responded to the new woman but his heart was dead within him.

In the early hours one morning he was smoking his chillum when an old friend happened to pass by. 'Ho, Bhavani, where are you going so early in the morning?'

Bhavani stopped. He had a small bundle on his shoulder. 'Nowhere in particular,' he said evasively.

'You should be on your way to some place or the other,' exclaimed Manak. 'What about a smoke?'

Bhavani sat down on his haunches and took the chillum from Manak's hands. 'I'm going to Chamba for the fair,' he said at last.

Bhavani's words pierced through Manak's heart like a needle. 'Is the fair today?'

'It's the same day, every year,' replied Bhavani drily. 'Don't you remember, we were in the same party seven years ago?' Bhavani did not say any more but Manak was conscious of the other man's rebuke and he felt uneasy. Bhavani put down the chillum and picked up his bundle. His flute was sticking out of the bundle. Manak's eye remained on the flute till Bhavani disappeared from view.

Next morning, Manak was in his fields when he saw Bhavani coming back but he looked the other way deliberately. He did not want to talk to Bhavani to hear anything about the fair. But Bhavani came round the other side and sat down in front of Manak. His face was sad and grey as a cinder.

'Guleri is dead,' Bhavani said in a flat voice.

'What?'

'When she heard of your second marriage, she soaked her clothes in kerosene and set fire to them.'

Manak, mute with pain, could only stare and feel his own life burning out.

The days went by. Manak resumed his work in the fields and ate his meals when they were given to him. But he was like a dead man, his face blank, his eyes empty.

'I am not his wife,' complained his second wife. 'I'm just someone he happened to marry.'

But quite soon she was pregnant and Manak's mother was pleased with her new daughter-in-law. She told Manak about his wife's condition, but he looked as if he did not understand and his eyes were still empty.

His mother encouraged her daughter-in-law to bear with her husband's moods for a few days. As soon as the child was born and placed in his father's lap, she said, Manak would change.

A son was duly born to Manak's wife; and his mother, rejoicing, bathed the boy, dressed him in fine clothes and put him in Manak's lap. Manak stared at the new-born babe in his lap. He stared a long time, uncomprehending, his face as usual expressionless. Then suddenly the blank eyes filled with horror and Manak began to scream. 'Take him away!' he shrieked hysterically, 'Take him away! He stinks of kerosene.'

Amrita Pritam

Glossary: *charpoy* – wooden-framed, string-laced bed
chillum/hookah – Eastern smoking pipes
dupattas – garment worn around the neck

Vendetta

Paolo Saverini's widow dwelt alone with her son in a small, mean house on the ramparts of Bonifacio. Built on a spur of the mountain and in places actually overhanging the sea, the town looks across the rockstrewn straits to the low-lying coast of Sardinia. On the other side, girdling it almost completely, there is a fissure in the cliff, like an immense corridor, which serves as a port, and down this long channel, as far as the first houses, sail the small Italian and Sardinian fishing boats, and once a fortnight the broken-winded old steamer from Ajaccio. Clustered together on the white hill-side, the houses form a patch of even more dazzling whiteness. Clinging to the rock, gazing down upon those deadly straits where scarcely a ship ventures, they look like the nests of birds of prey. The sea and the barren coast, stripped of all but a scanty covering of grass, are for ever harassed by a restless wind, which sweeps along the narrow funnel, ravaging the banks on either side. In all directions the black points of innumerable rocks jut out from the water, with trails of white foam streaming from them, like torn shreds of linen, floating and fluttering on the surface of the waves.

The widow Saverini's house was planted on the very edge of the cliff, and its three windows opened upon this wild and dreary prospect. She lived there with her son Antoine and their dog Sémillante, a great gaunt brute of the sheep-dog variety, with a long, rough coat, which the young man took with him when he went out shooting.

One evening, Antoine Saverini was treacherously stabbed in a quarrel by Nicolas Ravolati, who escaped that same night to Sardinia.

At the sight of the body, which was brought home by passersby, the old mother shed no tears, but she gazed long and silently at her dead son. Then, laying her wrinkled hand upon the corpse, she promised him the vendetta. She would not allow any one to remain with her, and shut herself up with the dead body. The dog Sémillante, who remained with her, stood at the foot of the bed and howled, with her head stretched out towards her master and her tail between her legs. Neither of them stirred, neither the dog nor the old mother, who was now leaning over the body, gazing at it fixedly, and silently shedding great tears. Still wearing his rough jacket, which was pierced and torn at the breast, the boy lay on his back as if asleep, but there was blood all about him, on his shirt, which had been stripped off in order to expose the wound, on his waistcoat and his trousers, face and hands. His beard and hair were matted with clots of blood.

The old mother began to talk to him, and at the sound of her voice the dog stopped howling.

'Never fear, never fear, you shall be avenged, my son, my little son, my poor child. You may sleep in peace. You shall be avenged, I tell you. You have your mother's word, and you know she never breaks it.'

Slowly she bent down and pressed her cold lips to the dead lips of her son.

Sémillante resumed her howling, uttering a monotonous, long-drawn wail, heart-rending and terrible. And thus the two remained, the woman and the dog, till morning.

The next day Antoine Saverini was buried, and soon his name ceased to be mentioned in Bonifacio.

. . . . .

He had no brother, nor any near male relation. There was no man in the family who could take up the vendetta. Only his mother, his old mother, brooded over it.

From morning till night she could see, just across the straits, a white speck upon the coast. This was the little Sardinian village of Longosardo, where the Corsican bandits took refuge whenever the hunt for them grew too hot. They formed almost the entire population of the hamlet. In full view of their native shores they waited for a chance to return home and take to the *maquis* again. She knew that Nicolas Ravolati had sought shelter in that village.

All day long she sat alone at her window gazing at the opposite coast and thinking of her revenge, but what was she to do with no one to help her, and she herself so feeble and near her end? But she had promised; she had sworn by the dead body of her son; she could not forget, and she dared not delay. What was she to do? She could not sleep at night, she knew not a moment of rest or peace, but racked her brains unceasingly. Sémillante, asleep at her feet, would now and then raise her head and emit a piercing howl. Since her master had disappeared, this had become a habit; it was as if she were calling him, as if she, too, were inconsolable and preserved in her canine soul an ineffaceable memory of the dead.

One night, when Sémillante began to whine, the old mother had an inspiration of savage, vindictive ferocity. She thought about it till morning. At daybreak she rose and betook herself to church. Prostrate on the stone floor, humbling herself before God, she besought Him to aid and support her, to lend to her poor, worn-out body the strength she needed to avenge her son.

Then she returned home. In the yard stood an old barrel with one end knocked in, which caught the rainwater from the eaves. She turned it over, emptied it, and fixed it to the ground with stakes and stones. Then she chained up Sémillante to this kennel and went into the house.

With her eyes fixed on the Sardinian coast, she walked restlessly up and down her room. He was over there, the murderer.

The dog howled all day and all night. The next morning the old woman brought her a bowl of water, but no food, neither soup nor bread. Another day passed. Sémillante was worn out and slept. The next morning her eyes were staring, and her coat gleaming, and she tugged frantically at her chain. And again the old woman gave her nothing to eat. Maddened with hunger Sémillante barked hoarsely. Another night went by.

At daybreak, the widow went to a neighbour and begged for two trusses of straw. She took some old clothes that had belonged to her husband, stuffed them with straw to represent a human figure, and made a head out of a bundle of old rags. Then, in front of Sémillante's kennel, she fixed a stake in the ground and fastened the dummy to it in an upright position.

The dog looked at the straw figure in surprise and, although she was famished, stopped howling.

The old woman went to the pork butcher and bought a long piece of black pudding. When she came home she lighted a wood fire in the yard, close to the kennel, and fried the black pudding. Sémillante bounded up and down in a frenzy, foaming at the mouth, her eyes fixed on the gridiron with its maddening smell of meat.

Her mistress took the steaming pudding and wound it like a cravat round the dummy's neck. She fastened it on tightly with string as if to force it inwards. When she had finished, she unchained the dog.

With one ferocious leap, Sémillante flew at the dummy's throat and, with her paws on its shoulders, began to tear it. She fell back with a portion of her prey between her jaws, sprang at it again, slashing at the string with her fangs, tore away some scraps of food, dropped for a moment, and hurled herself at it in renewed fury. She tore away the whole face with savage rendings and reduced the neck to shreds.

Motionless and silent, with burning eyes, the old woman looked on. Presently she chained the dog up again. She starved her another two days, and then put her through the same strange performance. For three months she accustomed her to this method of attack, and to tear her meals away with her fangs. She was no longer kept on the chain. At a sign from her mistress, the dog would fly at the dummy's throat.

She learned to tear it to pieces even when no food was concealed about its throat. Afterwards as a reward she was always given the black pudding her mistress had cooked for her.

As soon as she caught sight of the dummy, Sémillante quivered with excitement and looked at her mistress, who would raise her finger and cry in a shrill voice, 'Tear him!'

. . . . .

One Sunday morning when she thought the time had come, the widow Saverini went to confession and communion, in an ecstasy of devotion. Then she disguised herself like a tattered old beggar man, and struck a bargain with a Sardinian fisherman, who took her and her dog across to the opposite shore.

She carried a large piece of black pudding wrapped in a cloth bag. Sémillante had been starved for two days, and her mistress kept exciting her by letting her smell the savoury food.

The pair entered the village of Longosardo. The old woman hobbled along to a baker and asked for the house of Nicolas Ravolati. He had resumed his former occupation, which was that of a joiner, and he was working alone in the back of his shop.

The old woman threw open the door and called:

'Nicolas! Nicolas!'

He turned round. Slipping the dog's lead, she cried:

'Tear him! Tear him!'

The maddened animal flew at his throat. The man flung out his arms and grappled with the brute, and they rolled on the ground together. For some moments he struggled, kicking the floor with his feet. Then he lay still, while Sémillante tore his throat to shreds.

Two neighbours, seated at their doors, remembered to have seen an old beggar man emerge from the house and at his heels, a lean black dog, which was eating, as it went along, some brown substance that its master was giving it.

By the evening the old woman had reached home again.

That night she slept well.

Guy de Maupassant

Acknowledgements

The publishers wish to thank the following for their kind permission to reproduce copyright material:

Copyright Text:

Selima Hill: p41 *The Flowers* by Selima Hill from *Trembling Hearts in the Bodies of Dogs; New and Selected Poems*, Bloodaxe Books, 1994.

Ted Hughes: p35 *Wind* from *Hawk in the Rain* © Ted Hughes, reproduced by permission of Faber and Faber Ltd; p36 *The Thought-Fox* from *Hawk in the Rain* © Ted Hughes, reproduced by permission of Faber and Faber Ltd; p37 *The Stag* from *Season Songs* © Ted Hughes, reproduced by permission of Faber and Faber Ltd; p38 *Roe-Deer* from *Moortown* © Ted Hughes, reproduced by permission of Faber and Faber Ltd.

Jenny Joseph: p29 *Warning* © Jenny Joseph from *Selected Poems*, Bloodaxe Books, 1992, reproduced by permission of John Johnson Ltd, on behalf of the author.

Jackie Kay: p3 *Yellow* © Jackie Kay, reproduced by kind permission of Bloomsbury Children's Books; p4 *Brendon Gallacher* © Jackie Kay, reproduced by kind permission of Bloomsbury Children's Books; p5 *Lucozade* © Jackie Kay, reproduced by kind permission of Bloomsbury Children's Books; p39 *Keeping Orchids* © Jackie Kay, reproduced by kind permission of Bloomsbury Children's Books.

Philip Larkin: p30 *At Grass*, © Philip Larkin, The Marvell Press.

Christopher Logue: p14 an extract from *War Music*, reproduced by permission of Faber and Faber Ltd.

Adewale Maja-Pearce: pp72–74 *Veronica* © Adewale Maja-Pearce.

Guy de Maupassant: pp89–91 *Vendetta* © Guy de Maupassant, Penguin Books.

Duncan McNeil: p63 'Sport in Schools' by Duncan McNeil © Duncan McNeil, Member of the Scottish Parliament for Greenock & Inverclyde, originally published in the *Greenock Telegraph*, Monday October 8 2001.

Edwin Muir: p33 *The Horses* © Edwin Muir, reproduced by permission of Faber and Faber Ltd.

Grace Nichols: p11 *Wherever I Hang* © Grace Nichols, reproduced by permission of Curtis Brown on behalf of the author; p38 *Iguana Memory* © Grace Nichols, reproduced by permission of Curtis Brown on behalf of the author.

Cherry Norton: p65 'Pay your children too much attention . . .' by Cherry Norton, *The Independent*, Thursday April 13 2000.

Cathy O'Dowd: pp58–59 an extract published in *The Guardian* from *Just for the Love of it* by Cathy O'Dowd, published by Free to Decide, 2000.

Gabriel Okara: p24 *Once Upon a Time* © Gabriel Okara published and reproduced by permission of Andre Deutsch (1987).

Wilfred Owen: p12 *The Send-off* and p13 *Dulce et Decorum Est* from *The Complete Poems and Fragments*, 1983.

Brian Patten: p45 *A Blade of Grass* © Brian Patten, 1981, from *Love Poems*, first published by George, Allan and Unwin, care of Rogers, Coleridge and White Ltd.

Gervase Phinn: pp50–54 an extract from *The Other Side of the Dale* (Michael Joseph, 1988) © Gervase Phinn, 1988, reproduced by permission of Penguin Books Ltd.

Sylvia Plath: p31 *Mirror* from *Collected Poems* © Sylvia Plath, reproduced by permission of Faber and Faber Ltd; p40 *Mushrooms* from *Collected Poems* © Sylvia Plath, reproduced by permission of Faber and Faber Ltd.

Amrita Pritam: pp86–88 *A Stench of Kerosene* written in Punjabi by Amrita Pritam, translated by Khushwant Singh (ed) and published in *Land of Five Rivers: Stories from the Punjab*, Jacio Publishing House, Bombay, 1965.

Reporters from the *Children's Express*: p66 'Smacking not the answer, say kids' © Children's Express, Northern Ireland.

Theodore Roethke: p42 *The Storm* © Theodore Roethke, reproduced by permission of Faber and Faber Ltd.

Isaac Rosenberg: p46 *Break of Day in the Trenches.*

Carole Satyamurti: p29 *I Shall Paint my Nails Red* © Carole Satyamurti from *Selected Poems*, Bloodaxe Books, 2000, reproduced by permission of Bloodaxe Books.

Vernon Scannell: p1 *Hide and Seek* © Vernon Scannell, reproduced by kind permission of the author; p43 *Nettles* © Vernon Scannell, reproduced by kind permission of the author.

Stanley Stewart: pp47–49 an edited extract from *In the Empire of Genghis Khan: A Journey among Nomads* © Stanley Stewart, reproduced by permission of HarperCollins Publishers.

Matthew Sweeney: p6 *The House* from *Upon the Roof*, reproduced by permission of Faber and Faber Ltd.

Mildred Taylor: pp79–85 *The Gold Cadillac* © Mildred Taylor, Penguin Putnam Inc.

Every effort has been made to trace copyright holders of material reproduced in this book. Any rights not acknowledged will be acknowledged in subsequent printings if notice is given to the publisher.